A GUIDE TO MALTESE COOKING

130 mouth-watering recipes
collected and tried out by
Francis Darmanin

"And when we had escaped, then we knew that the island was called Malta. But the inhabitants showed us no small courtesy. For kindling a fire, they refreshed us all…"

Acts of the Apostles Chapter xxviii

Copyright: Francis Darmanin, 27/2 Creche Street, Sliema SLM 09, Malta
Telephone: (00356) 21333846

Illustrations: Jack Dedomenico and Andrew Micallef
Photography: Francis Darmanin
Back cover photo: Zone Five Co. Ltd.
Layout by Details Design Ltd.
Printed in Malta at P.E.G. Ltd, San Gwann
ISBN: 99909-79-00-6
First published 1996
Reprinted 2003

WARNING: The publisher shall not be held responsible for any ailment (such as gout or indigestion) which may result from following any of the recipes contained in this book.

ABBREVIATIONS AND EXPLANATIONS

1 kilo	2.2 lbs
g	gram (1000g = 1 kilo)
1 oz	about 28g
1 lb	455g
1 glass	2 decilitres
1 cup	1.5 decilitres
1 decilitres	1/10 of a litre
1 litre	about 1 3/4 pints
cm	centimetre
mm	millimetre
1 inch	2.5 cm
Lm1 Maltese lira	100 cents

All recipes for 4-6 persons, depending on appetite.

CONTENTS

FOREWORD

I was lucky to be born into a family that loved cooking and eating. My mother, Rosa (née Caruana Galizia), was the daughter of a lawyer. He died when she was still a girl of nine. She had nine brothers and sisters and they lived in a very large house in Old Bakery Street in Valletta. Her mother, my grandmother, managed her household very well. Grandfather having left her a considerable estate, she could afford maids and even a cook. As a matter of fact she still had a wonderful cook, Pawla, till the day she died at the venerable age of 99 in 1971.

It seems as though the love of cooking and appreciation of good food is something contagious, and the whole family must have caught the disease. My aunt Therese is still an excellent hostess and cook as were Louise and Lily. My uncles all loved their food, as did their children, my many cousins.

A few years ago I published the first book on Maltese food in the German language. Following the success of this book, I was encouraged by family, friends and colleagues to have it translated into English. At first I was reluctant to do so since there already were several others on the market. However, I eventually realised that my book, because of its practical format and not least on account of the delightful sketches, was in a category of its own. I finally decided to take the plunge, and this is the result. I hope you enjoy it.

INTRODUCTION

When people ask me, *what is traditional Maltese food?*, I give the following answer: For any country or region, traditional food is the ingenious way the inhabitants of that place combine local seasonal produce to create dishes that are not only tasty, but that reflect the real character of the region they originate from. At the dawn of the 3rd millenium, high-technology food-preservation methods and world-wide travel and telecommunication systems have seen to it that many of the barriers that previously existed around food culture have been brought down.

I don't recall having even heard of pizza or burgers in Malta before the late '60s. Today's generation of Maltese probably knows more about this type of food than about many delicious traditional recipes such as *torta tal-lampuki* and *bigilla*. As the world gets an even smaller place and people of different cultures continue to intermix, the origins of traditional cuisines will become vaguer and vaguer.

Cookery books such as this one will be an important source for future historians and anthropologists who might want to trace the development of traditional cuisines. My aim of writing this book is however definitely not academical.

Most of the recipes in this book have been passed on to me by my mother. She has tried them all hundreds of times over. I felt that her knowledge, and over half a century of experience of Maltese cookery should not go wasted but be passed on for the benefit of others. I know that she always tried to make use of the ingredients available on the day. Her shopping whether for meat, fish or vegetables was done on a daily basis. Most modern housewives find this system no longer convenient and it is slowly being abandoned. With the amount of foodstuffs now being imported and the proliferation of fridges and freezers, cooking and eating solely fresh, local produce, will soon be a thing of the past.

The recipes contained in this book should therefore contain the essence of what one could well and truly call Maltese food. I have made an effort to include any dish which might fall into this category, and at the same time to exclude others of recent importation. In so doing, I have elected to insert just a couple of recipes which though not traditionally Maltese, have over the years, become family favourites.

Traditional recipes will of course vary, even from household to household. I do not think that one should try to judge if one recipe for a particular dish is superior to the other. What makes a traditional dish really special are not just the actual ingredients themselves and their quantities, but the feelings the particular dish conveys. Though a dozen Maltese housewives will have a dozen recipes for *ross il-forn*, the feelings evoked by the very mention of this dish will be the same amongst the twelve of them – feelings of home and good food, memories of childhood, emotions of closeness to one's roots.

Those who go through this collection of recipes will be happy to find not only that the tiny island of Malta does have its own cuisine, a cuisine strongly influenced by its position in the centre of this historical sea, but that the dishes are simple to prepare, and the results usually delicious.

A NOTE ON CERTAIN INGREDIENTS

Maltese idiom: tilef il-qaleb u l-gbejna.
Translation: he lost the cheese and the basket (in which the cheese is made); meaning, he lost all.

All ingredients used in Maltese cooking are easy to come by in most European countries. Further explanation is required however regards certain ingredients.

Ricotta is a white soft cheese, almost neutral to the taste, which is made daily in very large quantities by the local dairy. It is made by heating salted water with milk, the whole process of manufacture being beyond the scope of this book. I am assured that in the past, water used to be taken from the sea to make ricotta.
Ricotta is so popular with the Maltese housewife, not only because it is cheap, but also on account of its versatility. Seasoned with salt and pepper, it's the ideal filling for pies and *pastizzi*; because of its bland taste it goes well as a sweet too, such as for *kannoli*, where it is studded with candied peel and bits of chocolate. A chunk of ricotta is an excellent addition to a plate of vegetable soup, and does extremely well with pasta dishes, such as *ravjul* and *makkarunelli*.

Ricotta is available in many European countries today, even in the United Kingdom. In most recipes it can be substituted by cottage cheese, cream cheese, or a mixture of both.

6

Orange-blossom water is the non-alcoholic essence produced from the tiny aromatic flowers of the orange tree. In Malta it can be bought very cheaply in 300cc bottles. It is used in many sweet recipes, and a few drops added to black coffee, do enhance the flavour.

Bacon: for the recipes in this book use smoked streaky bacon.

Capers are the buds of the caper bush(*Capparis spinosa*) which grows wild on cliffs, rocks and walls. Before the buds bloom, in April and May, they are picked and placed in salted water for a few weeks. They are then drained and stored in jars with vinegar, in which they will keep for many months. They are used in different sauces, salads and for *hobz biz-zejt*. Capers are definitely one of the most important ingredients in Maltese cookery. Maltese capers are specially tasty, and a large jar can be bought for under Lm2.00.

Gbejniet are little round cheeses which used to be made of goats', but nowadays even with cows' milk. These are eaten either fresh or preserved, in which case they are first left out in an airy place to dry, and then pickled in jars with a little oil and some vinegar, or first strewn with black pepper. The peppered cheeses are called *gbejniet tal-bzar*.

Soups

Maltese idiom: min ihawwad fil-borma jkun jaf x'fiha.
Translation: he who stirs the pot knows what's in it.

Up to some years ago, if one entered a Maltese household of a morning, one would find the housewife standing at the kitchen table peeling vegetables and scraping the soil off potatoes on to an old newspaper. Somewhere in the background, on a gas or kerosene stove, there would have been a tightly covered pot on a very low flame. A soup would be cooking. Somehow between the lid and the pot, some steam would manage to escape, filling the room and the whole house with a most welcoming mouth-watering aroma.

Most of our soups are the result of long slow cooking; many, a meal in themselves.

Brodu tal-qafas tat-tigieg
Chicken carcass soup

What a recipe to start with, you might think! Every European country has a recipe for chicken soup, though chickens definitely do not taste as they once did. When I was still a child we often had Sunday lunch at my grandmother's Sliema house on Tower Road where she also had a very large garden at the back - this sounds like an extravagant luxury nowadays. Those beautiful old houses have all been pulled down now. Anyway, she always kept a few chickens in the garden - chickens which were fed on real food - bread and left-overs.

The children loved running after the chickens just after they(the chickens not the children) had their heads sliced off by the cook. Then, when the soup was served at table, they would quarrel over who was to get the tiny yolks which would still be inside the chicken, and which gave such a mellow flavour to the soup.

The carcass of a previously roast chicken or turkey, 1 carrot, 1 kohl rabi, 1 onion, a stick of celery, 1 lemon, a handful of rice or semolina, 6 eggs.

The recipe I'm giving here is a variation on the usual chicken soup theme. Here the carcass is used, together with the neck and giblets. These are covered with water, some salt added, and brought to the boil. At this point, the vegetables are added, whole or chopped. The soup is now simmered for 1 1/2 hours. Towards the end some rice or semolina can be added. The carcass is now removed, the chicken flesh taken off the skeleton and thrown back into the soup. If you like you can beat a raw egg in each soup bowl and slowly pour in the steaming soup. Or else just serve with lemon quarters. *An ideal way to cook left-over turkey on Boxing Day!*

BRODU TAT-TIGIEG BIL-HAXU
STUFFED-CHICKEN BROTH

The recipe for this soup is found on page 59, in the recipe for stuffed chicken. As in the previous recipe, the chicken broth can be had on its own with lemon wedges, or with some beaten egg. If you omit the eggs, a little sherry in each soup bowl definitely enhaces the taste.

BRODU TAL-LAHAM U TAL-MUDULUN
MEAT AND BONE-MARROW BROTH

Half a kilo of brisket, marrow bones, 1 kohl rabi, 1 carrot, 1 onion, 2 potatoes, tomato paste, small pasta shapes.

The meat which is cooked in this soup is usually served with green sauce (page 46) as the main dish, and accompanied by vegetables and potatoes which have been steamed on the soup pot. The meat together with a number of marrow bones are put into a pot, covered with water and brought to the boil.

The scum is removed and the vegetables are added. A dessertspoon of tomato paste is stirred in, and the soup simmered for 2 1/2 hours. Towards the end, a handful of small pasta shapes, bows or stars, are added. The meat is removed from the pot and reserved for later. The marrow is scooped out of the bones (there actually were spoons specially designed for this purpose) and spread onto fresh bread, sprinkled with freshly ground black or white pepper and eaten as an accompaniment to the soup. We used to sip the soup, leaving the pasta shapes at the bottom of our bowls. These were then sprinkled with grated cheese and devoured with great delight. No wonder the Maltese love a soup!

Brodu tal-Muntun
Barley soup with mutton
See page 49

Soppa tal-Ghazz bis-Saqajn tal-Majjal
Lentil soup with pigs trotters

An excellent soup for a cold winter's day.

1 carrot, 1 kohl rabi, 1 onion, 1 bay leaf, 1/4 kilo green lentils, 4 pork trotters and some pieces of shin of pork.

Rinse the lentils and soak them overnight. Drain, and add fresh water to the pot. Insert the well scrubbed pork trotters and the pork shin. Put in the bay leaf and a spoon of salt(but definitely not if using salted trotters!). Boil for half an hour and then add the vegetables cut up into chunks. Continue to simmer until the lentils are tender. Remove the trotters and meat, and serve on side plates. A knob of good butter and a little mustard can be stirred into each bowl for that extra zest.

Brodu ta l-Ilsien
Ox-tongue broth

An excellent broth is made with the tongue of an ox and root vegetables.

1 ox tongue or 2 pigs' tongues, 1 kohl rabi, 1 carrot, 1 onion, 1 small potato, a stick of celery, 1/2 a cup of raw rice.

Wash the tongue or tongues very well in salted water. Place in a pot, cover with water and bring slowly to the boil. Remove the scum and add the coarsely chopped vegetables. Simmer till the tongue is tender. Towards the end, add the rice. The tongue is now skinned and served with a delicious sauce (page 52).

KAWLATA
VEGETABLE AND SAUSAGE HOT-POT

The vegetables:1/4 kilo pumpkin, 1 kohl rabi, 4 carrots, 1/2 a cabbage, celery, 4 small potatoes, 2 onions. The meat: 1/2 kilo pork belly or gammon, or 6 Maltese sausages.

If using smoked or salted gammon, this must be soaked overnight whilst if using sausages, these should be fresh pork sausages.
Cover the meat or sausages with water, bring to the boil and remove any scum. Add all the vegetables which should be cut into largish chunks. Simmer gently until the meat is done. For a complete meal, remove the meat and cook some small macaroni beads in the soup for some 15 minutes.

KIRXA
TRIPE

The Maltese idiom *kilna il-kirxa flimkien*, translated literally "we ate tripe together", is used to describe a great degree of familiarity to or with some person - we were so familiar or such good friends, that we even used to eat tripe together! This of course also denotes the status that this dish must have once held - so much so, that two good friends would sit and reminisce over a plate of tripe!

1 kilo of tripe, 1/2 kilo pumpkin, 1/2 a cabbage, 1 cauliflower broken up into sprigs, 2 carrots, 2 onions, 3 thickly sliced potatoes, 1 kohl rabi, 1 lemon, some croutons.

First clean the tripe very well in lots of salted water, then rub it all over with lemon. Cut the tripe into 3cm strips, place in a large pot, cover with water and simmer for 1 hour. Now add the vegetables all cut into thick chunks or slices. Cook for a further 1 1/2 hours and serve with grated cheese and croutons. Indeed, this is more of a stew than a soup!

11

MINESTRA
VEGETABLE HOT-POT

1/2 kilo pumpkin, 1 kohl rabi, 2 carrots, 1 large onion, a stick of celery, 1/2 a small cauliflower, 2 potatoes, 1/4 of a cabbage head, 1 tablespoon of tomato paste, olive oil, pasta beads, seasoning, grated parmesan.

This is a thick vegetable soup, loved by all Maltese.
The pumpkin must be cut into chunks. This is the most important ingredient because of the lovely orange colour it gives to the soup. It is this warm colour which springs to mind when one thinks of *minestra*. These lovely pumpkins are harvested in summer but can be seen throughout autumn and winter on the roofs of the farmhouses where they have been left in rows to ripen in the sun. The rest of the vegetables, must be chopped into smaller pieces. Bring to the boil about 2 litres of water into which you have dissolved the tomato paste. Add all the vegetables, pour 2 tablespoons of olive oil over them and season with salt and pepper. When the water boils again, lower the heat and cook for 1 1/2 hours. Now add a handful of little pasta beads or small tubes. Cook for a further 15 minutes, and serve with grated cheese. This soup should be of a very thick consistency, unlike the Italian *minestrone*, which is much more watery.

SOPPA TA L-ARMLA
WIDOW'S SOUP

2 onions, 1 tablespoon tomato paste, 1 kohl rabi, 2 carrots, a stick of celery, 1 small cauliflower, 2 potatoes, 100g of both shelled peas and broad beans, 1/2 kilo spinach, 6 eggs, 250g ricotta or other type of fresh cheese, 100g sheeps' cheese, some croutons.

In the same pot in which you're making your soup, gently sautee the sliced onions in some olive oil. Add the tomato puree mixed with a tumbler of warm water, and stir it into the frying onions. Add the kohl rabi, the carrots, the celery, the cauliflower and the potatoes, all sliced or diced, and the peas and beans. Pour in enough water to cover, season, bring to the boil and reduce the heat. In the meantime wash the spinach, chop it up and add it about 15 minutes after the soup has boiled. Cook for a further hour. Before serving time, poach the eggs in the soup - one egg per person - which must not be boiling too vigorously. Using a slotted spoon remove the eggs and place one in each bowl, then ladle the soup over them. Pass around fresh ricotta cheese, pieces of goats' or sheeps' cheese, and the croutons, all to be added to the individual soup plates.

Soppa ta l-armla - Widow's soup

KUSKSU
SPRING SOUP

2 onions, 2 tablespoons tomato paste, 1 kilo of broad beans, 1 cup of shelled peas, kusksu beads, olive oil, grated parmesan.

This dish is eaten in spring and at Easter time, when broad beans are very much in season, and of course very cheap. It gets its name from the tiny pearls of pasta which are cooked in the soup and give it its particular consistency. These pasta pearls or beads can be found at most grocery stores and supermarkets, especially at that time of year when broad beans are in season (March to May). Maltese *kusksu* is not to be confused with the North African dish called *couscous*, which is rather different, though the name sounds similar.

Chop the onions and fry in oil and butter until they soften. Add the tomato paste and a glass of warm water, stir, and cook slowly. In the meantime shell the broad beans, and add them to the pan together with a cupful of peas. Add enough hot water to cover, and cook properly. When the peas are ready, add half a packet of *kusksu* beads, and cook for a further 20 minutes, by which time they should be ready. Serve with grated cheese. At Easter time children love having *kusksu*.

ALJOTTA
FISH SOUP

2 large onions, 10 cloves of garlic, 3 tomatoes, 1 teaspoon of tomato paste, a handful each of dried or fresh mint and marjoram, olive oil, 1 lemon, 1/2 cup of rice.

The Maltese word for fish soup *aljotta* derives from the Italian *aglio*, which actually means garlic - indeed a large amount of garlic, together with fresh fish and lots of herbs, is always used in this most wonderful soup.

You will require the head, tail, and fins of a large fish (say a grouper) which you are going to poach, or from a couple of smaller fish such as *lampuki* (my favourites), or else about half a dozen whole fish of a much smaller variety - scorpion fish, damsel fish or small bogue, are all ideal.

Chop up the onions and fry them slowly in oil. Add the whole garlic, plenty of fresh or dried marjoram and mint, the peeled and chopped tomatoes, and a teaspoon of tomato paste diluted in a cup of warm water. Cook slowly for 10 minutes. Now put in the fish (if small fish is used, clean very well). Cover just with water, season with salt, and cook for 1/2 an hour. Remove the fish, retaining any edible flesh for the soup and discarding the rest. Add more marjoram, and serve with lemon wedges. Towards the end of cooking time, you can also add half a cup of rice, or some left-over boiled rice. For those of you cooking this soup far away from the shores of the Mediterranean, do not hesitate to substitute with any type of fish from your region, as long as it is fresh. The addition of anything coming fresh from the sea, such as an octopus tentacle, and small crabs or sea anemones, can only enhance the flavour. This soup, however, is not meant to be one thick with fish, as the French *bouillabaisse*, but more of a savoury fish broth.

SOPPA TAL-QARA BAGHLI JEW QAR AHMAR
VEGETABLE MARROW OR PUMPKIN SOUP

This is a recipe for a creamy soup, in contrast to the thick vegetable soups of the preceding recipes.

1 kilo marrows (or pumpkin), 2 onions, 2 potatoes, some croutons.

Sautee the sliced onions in butter for a few minutes. Add the coarsely chopped marrows and potatoes. Give the marrows a quick fry and add enough hot water (or, preferably, beef or chicken stock) to cover, and allow to simmer till the vegetables are done. Let the soup cool down slightly, season to taste with salt, pepper, and a hint of grated nutmeg, and liquidize in an electric blender. Serve with the croutons. You can substitute the marrow with pumpkin if you like or make half and half!

15

SOPPA TAT-TADAM
TOMATO SOUP

This is a summer soup and is made from large and juicy field tomatoes that have an almost sweet and sour flavour.

1 onion, 1 kilo ripe tomatoes, a stick of celery, salt, some croutons.

Sautee the sliced onion in olive oil; add the chopped tomatoes and celery, season with salt, and cook till the tomatoes are soft. Now pass everything through a sieve adding water as you go along. Season with salt and serve with the croutons.

Maltese saying: L-ewwel ma tiekol, l-ghajn.
Translation: The first to eat is the eye; meaning, if a dish is nicely presented, it will be more appetizing.

Pasta, Rice and Savoury Pies

On account of the historical and geographical closeness to the island of Sicily you will notice in some of the recipes in this section, similarities to certain Sicilian regional specialities. Though such resemblances are inevitable, I have omitted all recent importations, such as pizza and lasagne, and included only recipes like *ross il-forn*, *timpana*, and others which are without doubt typically Maltese, or at least local innovations of what once might have been a foreign (Sicilian) dish. Pasta, as can be seen by the large number of *pizzerie* and pasta houses springing up all over the place, is much loved by the Maltese. Many workers eat a cheap lunch of *timpana* or *mqarrun* (macaroni) as a snack during their lunch break, whilst at home, pasta is very often the starter to the meal, even at Christmas time, when traditional roast turkey is preceeded in many homes by, once again, *timpana*, or, nowadays, lasagne!

Our pasta dishes are more than just boiled spaghetti served with a sauce; as you will see, many of them are baked dishes - all equally satisfying and tasty.

From a Maltese folk song: meta ommi kella lili, ghamlet ir-ross il-forn.
Translation: On the day that I was born, my mother made ross il-forn.

Ross il-forn
Baked Rice

The most appetizing aroma of a dish of *ross il-forn* just come out of the oven, is known and loved by every Maltese.

You need: 400g raw rice, 400g minced pork, 2 chopped chicken livers, 2 diced onions, 3 eggs, 2 heaped tablespoons grated cheese, 1 tablespoon tomato paste, some saffron.

Sweat the onions in some pork fat or oil, add the mince and chicken livers, season, pour in the tomato paste mixed with a little water, and allow to simmer very gently for 1 hour. Mix the raw rice with the sauce and pour into a large buttered pyrex dish. Stir in the grated cheese. In the meantime soak a few saffron threads in warm water (double the volume of rice e.g. 2 cups rice, 4 cups water) and add to the dish. Beat the eggs lightly and pour on top of everything. Bake in a moderate oven without stirring for about 90 minutes. The eggs form a soft spongy layer on top, beneath which will be the savoury, crispy, yellow coloured rice.

Incidentally, the Maltese word for yellow is *safra*. The saffron crocus has been observed growing wild in certain places in Malta in autumn. It is surprising that no local entrepeneur has thought of cultivating this plant, considering how expensive it is to buy.

Timpana
Macaroni in pastry parcel

This is a famous and very popular dish. It is not only delicious but also very satisfying, and eaten by thousands of Maltese workers every day as a snack in the cafes and cheaper restaurants. This is how you make it:

For 6 servings you need 1/2 kilo of puff pastry, 1/2 kilo macaroni, 1/4 kilo minced pork and the same of minced beef, 2 finely chopped onions, 1 aubergine - sliced, salted and drained, 2 hard-boiled eggs, 2 raw, beaten eggs, 4 tablespoons tomato paste, 4 tablespoons grated cheese.

18

Fry the onions in oil or fat. Before they get brown, add the minced meats and stir-fry. Season with pepper and salt, and pour in the diluted tomato paste. Stir well and simmer at least 1 1/2 hours, adding more liquid if necessary. Meanwhile boil the macaroni for about 7 minutes in salted water without letting them get soft (overboiled). Drain the macaroni and mix into the sauce. Add 2 tablespoons of the cheese, and the beaten eggs. Mix well and add the rest of the cheese. Dust the aubergine slices with flour, and fry them in hot vegetable oil.

Line a deep baking dish with the pastry, reserving some for the cover. Pour in half of the macaroni/sauce mixture, add the quartered hard-boiled eggs and thin slices of fried aubergine. Top up with more macaroni, and finally cover with the pastry lid. Bake for 10 minutes in a hot oven, lower the heat, and bake for a further 45 minutes.

MAKKARUNELLI BL-IRKOTTA
MACARONI WITH RICOTTA CHEESE

For this recipe we use a thicker type of what I call corrugated macaroni which is known as *makkarunelli*.

1/2 kilo macaroni or similar type of pasta, 2 eggs, 1/2 kilo fresh ricotta cheese, a cupful of parsley, butter, seasoning, grated parmesan.

Boil 1/2 kilo of these *makkarunelli* (or macaroni) in salted water, and drain in a colander. Allow 2 tablespoons of butter to melt in a saucepan. Meanwhile beat the eggs and pour them over the ricotta cheese in a bowl. To this add the chopped parsley, freshly ground pepper, and salt, mashing well into the ricotta-egg mixture. Transfer the drained *makkarunelli* to the saucepan with the molten butter, add the ricotta, and heat slowly over a very low fire. Serve with a plain tomato and garlic sauce and sprinkle liberally with grated cheese.

RAVJUL
RICOTTA-FILLED PASTA POCKETS

These are small pasta pockets or cases, which are filled with savoury ricotta cheese, boiled and served with a juicy tomato sauce. Maltese *ravjul* are much larger than the Italian *ravioli*, which are usually only about one quarter of the size of their local counterparts.

For the filling: 400g ricotta, 2 raw eggs, 3 tablespoons grated cheese, a large bunch of chopped parsley, seasoning.

For the dough: 400g plain flour, salt, 2 egg yolks, a little oil.

To make the dough: Sieve the flour together with a teaspoon of salt into a basin. Add the egg-yolks and rub together between your fingers, adding 4 tablespoons of vegetable oil and a little warm water. Knead the pastry well, and let it rest for about 1 hour. Divide the pastry into two, rolling out one of the halves, so that it lies flat on the table in a square shape about 3mm thick. In the meanwhile prepare the filling: Mix together the ricotta, the eggs, the grated cheese, the chopped parsley, lots of ground black pepper and salt. Now, take tablespoons of the spicy ricotta filling, and pile them up in rows on your flattened pastry square, each a few centimetres apart. Gently lower the other pastry half, pressing and sealing firmly around each separate pile of ricotta. Finally, cut out the individual *ravjul*. Now boil the *ravjul* in plenty of salted water until just done. Serve with tomato sauce flavoured with garlic and basil, and sprinkle with grated cheese. *Ravjul*, which the children love, are ideal for deep freezing. Cook frozen *ravjul* by simmering gently for about 20 minutes.
The restaurants usually serve *ravjul* in portions of a dozen. Left-over *ravjul* can be kept in the fridge and are ideal as a snack fried in oil.

RAVJUL MOQLI
FRIED RAVIOLI

Any *ravjul* left over from the previous recipe are kept in the fridge and eaten as a light lunch one or two days later.
Pour some vegetable oil into a wide pan. When the oil gets hot, put in the previously cooked, cold *ravioli*, and fry till crisp and golden brown. Remove with a slotted spoon and serve immediately. If you have a sweet tooth, you can sprinkle the *ravioli* with some sugar.

20

Zalza tat-tadam bil-qara baghli w bringiel
Sauce for spaghetti with marrows and aubergines

In summertime in Malta there is always an abundance of aubergines and marrows. The most is made of these, even in such simple dishes as spaghetti with tomato sauce. A plain tomato sauce is prepared (according to your own favourite recipe), and served with the pasta. Plenty of parmesan cheese is sprinkled over it and slices of marrows or aubergines, fried quite brown, are placed on top. Aubergine slices have to be soaked in salted water for 1/2 hour, and then drained before frying. The crispy vegetables make all the difference to this simple dish.

Mqarrun il-forn
Baked macaroni

This may seem to be just another pasta and meat-sauce recipe - but it's different. It's easy to prepare beforehand, and so tasty, that you will soon realise why *mqarrun* is such a favourite workman's lunch.

1/2 kilo macaroni, 1/2 kilo mixed pork and beef mince, 2 onions, 2 beaten eggs, 2 tablespoons tomato paste, 4 tablespoons grated parmesan, salt and pepper, oil for frying.

Lightly fry the finely chopped onions till golden, add the minced meat, allow it to brown, and season with salt and lots of ground pepper. Mix the tomato paste with a tumbler of warm water, pour into the pan with the meat, and cook slowly for about 1 hour. In the meantime parboil the macaroni in salted water, making sure you leave them slightly hard to the bite. Drain the macaroni and transfer them to a large bowl. After the macaroni has cooled somewhat, mix it well with the eggs and 3 tablespoons of the cheese. When the meat sauce is ready, add this too, mixing thoroughly, and then transfer everything to a buttered ovenproof dish. Sprinkle with the rest of the grated cheese and bake on medium for about half an hour. The macaroni at the top of the dish should become quite dark and crunchy.

Mqarrun mahmug
Dirty macaroni

1/2 kilo macaroni, 1/2 kilo mixed pork and beef mince, 2 onions, 1 hard-boiled egg, 1 aubergine or marrow, 2 tablespoons tomato paste, 4 tablespoons grated parmesan, salt and pepper, oil for frying.

21

Parboil the macaroni so that it is still slightly hard to the bite. Cut the aubergine into little cubes, sprinkle with salt and allow to drain in a colander, then fry in olive oil, browning all over. Sweat the sliced onions in lard or oil, adding the mince and the tomato paste mixed with warm water. Let this sauce bubble for about 20 minutes. Now mix the macaroni with the fried aubergine dices, the chopped egg and the meat sauce. Sprinkle with the grated cheese.

Ghagin grieg
Greek pasta

How did this dish get its name? Who knows? My mother borrowed the recipe 40 years ago from a neighbour, and it's been a family favourite ever since. Indeed it is an effortless and extremely tasty pasta dish. The type of pasta to be used should be small 1cm to 2cm beads, though larger macaroni, or pasta shells would do as well.

1/2 kilo pasta, 600g good pork mince which must not be too fatty, 2 bacon rashers, 3 onions, butter, a chicken cube, grated cheese, seasoning.

Slice the onions very thinly, chop the bacon finely and place them with the minced pork into a wide pan. Pour in enough water just to cover the meat, crush the chicken cube and sprinkle onto the meat, season well with ground black pepper and a little salt. Finally add a large knob of good butter. Cover and leave on the lowest flame possible. After about two hours, the sauce, which will be pale in colour, will be ready. In the meantime boil the pasta till it is just done, drain, and return to the pot. Pour the sauce over the pasta, and finally stir in the cheese. Mix well to coat all of the pasta with the creamy meat sauce.

Torta tas-spinaci, qlub tal-qaqocc u ncova
Spinach, artichoke-heart and anchovy pie

For the filling: 1/2 a kilo spinach, 2 onions, 6 tomatoes, 8 artichoke hearts, 150g shelled peas, 100g salted-anchovy fillets, 2 hard-boiled eggs.

For the pastry: 200g plain flour, 100g margarine, 1 egg, salt.

Make a shortcrust pastry by rubbing the flour into the fat, and then adding the salt, the egg, and enough water necessary to make a stiff dough. Let it rest for 1 hour, and in the meantime prepare the filling.

First boil, drain, and chop the spinach. Then fry the chopped onions in olive oil, add the peeled and sliced tomatoes, the quartered artichoke hearts and the peas, and cook slowly. When soft, lift the artichokes out of the pan, and put in the spinach and anchovy fillets instead. Mix well, and cook for a few minutes further. Line a baking dish with the pastry, and spread it with the filling, adding the artichoke hearts with the halved hard-boiled eggs on top. Cover with a pastry lid, prick with a fork, and bake in a moderate oven until the pastry is crisp and golden.

TORTA TAL-FENEK
RABBIT PIE

Any left overs from a *fenkata* (page 61), can be made into this delightful pie. For a pie of medium size, you require:

250g shortcrust pastry, pieces of fried or stewed rabbit, 1 onion, 2 cloves of garlic, a piece of smoked bacon (about 150g), 1 small aubergine, 1 large marrow, 4 peeled tomatoes, a handful of peas, oil for frying, 1/2 a teaspoon of curry powder.

Dice the aubergine, the onion, the marrow, and the pork or bacon. Start off by sprinkling the aubergine cubes with salt, and putting them in a colander, allowing them to give off some of their bitter juices. In the meantime take the previously cooked rabbit pieces and remove the meat from the bones. Now fry all the cubed vegetables and the garlic in hot oil, without overcooking. Remove them from the pan and put aside; now brown the bacon in the same oil, add the chopped tomatoes, stir, and cook for about 5 minutes. Return the fried vegetables to the pan, together with the peas and the chopped up rabbit meat. Season with the curry powder, salt and ground black pepper, and cook till the peas are done. Line a round pie dish with the pastry, spread it evenly with the filling, cover with a pastry lid, prick with a fork, and bake in a medium oven for about 35 minutes.

TORTA TAL-MAJJAL BIL-QAR AHMAR
PUMPKIN AND PORK TART

For a largish pie: 500g puff pastry, 600g pumpkin, 300g rice, 225g pork, 2 onions, 1/2 a teaspoon caraway seeds, seasoning.

Boil the rice in salted water and allow to drain. Toss and fry the finely chopped onions with the finely diced pork in hot olive oil, browning well all over. Cut up the pumpkin into large cubes, add to the pan, and allow everything to simmer in the pumpkin's juices till tender. Remove from the flame, mix with the cooked rice and season with the crushed caraway seeds, salt and pepper. Line a shallow pie dish with half of the pastry, spread the filling evenly on top and cover with a lid made from the rest of the pastry. Prick with a fork, and bake for half an hour in a medium oven.

QASSATA TAL-QAR AHMAR, TONN U NCOVA
TUNA, ANCHOVY, AND PUMPKIN PIE

For a pie of average size: 350g pastry, 1 cup of raw rice, 400g pumpkin, 200g tinned tuna, 2 leeks, 10 anchovy fillets, 8 chopped black olives, a small handful of currants, a glass of white wine, a pinch of nutmeg, black pepper, olive oil.

Cut up the leeks, and fry them in oil in a large pan. Add the raw rice and stir-fry for some minutes. Add the pumpkin cut into cubes, and pour in the wine. Cover and allow to cook on a slow fire till the pumpkin is tender. Chop the anchovy fillets, and together with the flaked tuna fish, the olives and the currants, stir into the rice/pumpkin mixture. Season to taste with a little salt, ground black pepper and grated nutmeg. Line a pie dish with pastry, spread evenly with the stuffing, and seal with a pastry lid. Now prick, and bake for about 1 hour in a moderate oven.

TORTA TAL-FUL U RIKOTTA
BEAN AND RICOTTA TART

350 g shortcrust or puff pastry, 2 eggs, 1 kilo broad beans, 500g ricotta, about 100g sheeps' cheese, 2 tablespoons grated parmesan, 2 small onions, 6 medium sized tomatoes, 1 teaspoon thyme, a little olive oil for frying.

Fry the finely diced onions in olive oil till golden, add the chopped tomatoes, cook slowly for 25 minutes, inserting the shelled beans towards the end. Sprinkle with some thyme. In a large bowl mash the ricotta with the chopped sheeps' cheese, the grated cheese and the beaten eggs. Now pour in the tomato/bean sauce and blend very well. Line a round pie dish with pastry, spread evenly with the filling, and cover with a pastry lid. Brush with egg yolk, prick several times with a fork and bake in a medium oven for 30 to 40 minutes. Allow to cool, and serve. Very good cold.

TORTA TAR-RIKOTTA W SPINACI
SPINACH AND RICOTTA PIE

For 2 medium sized pies: 1/2 kilo short or puff pastry, 1 kilo spinach, 1 kilo ricotta, 100g grated parmesan, 2 fresh Maltese cheeselets (or 100g sheeps' cheese), 2 eggs, a bunch of parsley, nutmeg and seasoning.

Wash, cook, drain and chop the spinach. In the meantime mash the ricotta with the sheeps' cheese, the beaten eggs and the spices. Mix in the prepared spinach. Grease 2 baking tins, and line the sides and bottom of each with the pastry. Fill with the savoury ricotta/spinach mixture, cover with pastry lids, prick with a fork, and bake in a hot oven, first for 10 minutes, and then for a further 45 minutes at reduced temperature. Allow to cool before serving. Also good cold.

PASTIZZI
CHEESECAKES

Pastizzi or cheesecakes as they are also known in English, are those delightful puff-pastry pockets filled with savoury ricotta cheese or with vegetables, usually peas, and which are such a favourite with the Maltese. They are made at special confectioneries called *pastizzeriji*, from where they are transported on huge black trays, hot from the oven at regular intervals, to the various bars and cafes, where they are sold for only a few cents each. Every village has its *pastizzerija*, some have several. Certain localities such as Qormi and Rabat have a reputation for first class *pastizzi*, and people will come from miles away to get their *pastizzi* from a renowned *pastizzerija*. Loved by rich and poor alike, the ideal workman's breakfast, lunch, or snack, always a popular item at every wedding or baptism celebration, *pastizzi* are truly a part of local tradition.

Even in Toronto, Canada, where there is a large Maltese community, there have sprung up a couple of Maltese style *pastizzeriji*.
Since the making of genuine *pastizzi* requires a lot of skill and experience, not least because of the unique shape into which the pastry has to be twisted, I have decided to give recipes for

25

pastizzotti or small *pastizzi* which are much easier to make at home and also just as popular at parties and feasts.

PASTIZZOTTI TAR-RIKOTTA
LITTLE CHEESECAKES

3/4 kilo puff pastry, 400g ricotta cheese, 2 eggs, 2 tablespoons grated cheese, lots of chopped parsley, freshly ground black pepper.

Mash the ricotta with the beaten eggs. Mix in the herbs and spices. Roll out the pastry thinly, cut out circles about 9cm in diameter, and place a spoonful of the mixture onto each of these. Fold each pastry circle in half around the filling and press the edges firmly together. Place on a greased baking tray and bake in a hot oven for circa 1/2 an hour or till the pastry is done. This recipe should give you about 30 *pastizzotti*.

PASTIZZOTTI TAL-BRINGIEL
LITTLE AUBERGINE-FILLED PIES

3/4 kilo shortcrust pastry, 2 onions, 1 large aubergine, 2 large tomatoes, 6 olives, 6 salted-anchovy fillets, 3 hard-boiled eggs, marjoram and basil.

Cut the aubergine into thick cubes, sprinkle with salt and put aside for half an hour. Fry the diced onions in olive oil, add the drained aubergine pieces, and continue frying gently. Add the chopped tomatoes and olives, and finally the herbs. Cook until the aubergine cubes are soft. Roll out the pastry thinly, cut out circles about 9cm in diameter, and pile the mixture in spoonfuls onto the pastry circles. Place a little piece of egg and of anchovy fillet on each pile of filling and proceed to fold as in the preceding recipe.

PASTIZZOTTI TAL-MOHH
LITTLE BRAIN-FILLED PIES

3/4 kilo short-crust pastry, 1/2 an ox brain or 3 pigs' brains, 1 onion, 2 slices of ham or 2 bacon rashers, a cup of peas, a bunch of parsley, nutmeg, salt and pepper.

First soak the brains in salted water for 1 hour, remove their outer skin, drain in a colander and cut into small pieces. Poach the brains, together with a finely chopped onion, the ham or bacon sliced into thin strips, the peas, and a knob of good butter, in a shallow pan with a little water. When the brains are almost done, season with salt, freshly ground pepper and a pinch of nutmeg, and sprinkle with chopped parsley. Pour off any excess liquid, as you don't want the mixture to be too runny. Now make the *pastizzotti* as in the 2 previous recipes.

TORTA TAL-LAMPUKI JEW TONN
LAMPUKI OR TUNA FISH PIE

This most delicious of pies is made in the months of September to December, when the popular fish *lampuki* (singular *lampuka*), are in season and very cheap. *Lampuki* is only caught in certain parts of the Mediterranean; the colour of the fish is a lovely iridescent blue with splashes of emerald green, the silvery sides speckled with deep blue and yellow spots; the taste of a fresh *lampuka* fried in good oil and served just with a squeeze of lemon is exquisite; I would describe it as the taste of the sea. If you happen to be in Malta during the *lampuki* season, do not neglect to try fresh *lampuki* in one of our many fish restaurants. Refuse *lampuki* if they are served to you between March and July. They will definitely not be fresh; frozen *lampuki* is inferior both in taste and consistency. When *lampuki* is out of season, this pie is made with tinned tuna fish. It is an excellent substitute and easier to make. You can make tuna-fish pie wherever you are in the world, I'm sure you won't be disappointed. It's definitely one of my favourite dishes.

To make 2 medium sized pies: About 400g shortcrust pastry, 2 kilos spinach, 200g peas, 1 tin peeled tomatoes, 1 small cauliflower, a dozen olives, 3 hard-boiled eggs, 1 onion, a handful of sultanas, 4 potatoes, 1 large tin of tuna fish.

Wash, cook, drain, and chop the spinach. Parboil the potatoes and slice them very thinly. Cook the cauliflower and separate into florets. Sautee the sliced onion in olive oil, add the tomatoes and the peas, season with salt and pepper, cover, and simmer for a few minutes. To this now add the cauliflower florets and the spinach and cook on a low flame for a further 10 minutes. Finally mix in the sultanas, the stoned and chopped olives and the flaked tuna, remove from the fire and allow to cool. Roll out the pastry. Line 2 greased pie dishes with a pastry bottom, and arrange a layer of potato slices on each; spread the mixture evenly on top of the potatoes, and distribute the hard-boiled egg slices equally between the two pies. Cover with pastry lids, prick with a fork, and brush with oil. Start baking in a high oven, and then lower the heat. Let the pies cool down before serving. They can also be served cold with a little olive oil dribbled over them. You can also use the same recipe for making miniature pies, which are ideal as party snacks.

Maltese idiom: tfittex ix-xaghra fl-ghagina
Translation: to look for a hair in the dough; meaning, to do one's best to find a fault with
someone or something

VEGETABLES AND SALADS

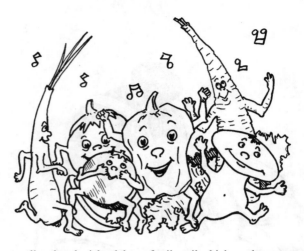

Malta, though a small and rocky island, has a fertile soil which produces two separate crops of a variety of vegetables a year. This, coupled with the fact that our vegetables are of a high quality, and cheap when in season, makes them a very important and popular item on the menu. A number of vegetable vendors visit the towns and villages every day, some of them taking up prominent positions on the main streets or squares.

It is from one of these that the Maltese housewife does her daily shopping for vegetables. Although there are fixed government- controlled retail prices for fresh vegetables, there will always be an amount of bargaining at the vegetable van, as the housewife chooses carefully and feels every vegetable that she picks, making sure that it's just right for the dish she is preparing. In summertime there will be an abundance of tomatoes for *hobz biz-zejt*, a favourite snack; lovely, shiny aubergines for baking; huge marrows for stuffing and poaching in broth; green and red peppers for *kapunata*, to be eaten with fish.

In winter, enormous pumpkins which for months have been ripening on some farmhouse roof, are now being cut up and sold by the slice to go into *minestra* and other soups. Beans, artichokes, and cauliflower are at their best and cheapest, and they will make excellent stews, on their own, with other vegetables, with meats, and even with fish. The vegetable lover will definitely not be disappointed in Maltese cookery.

Maltese idiom: Ghal habba bzar tilef il-borma.
Meaning: Spoil not the dish for a pennyworth of pepper.

Bringiel Mimli il-Forn
Baked Aubergines with Potatoes

3 aubergines, 1 onion, 400g minced meat(pork and beef), 2 beaten eggs, 2 tablespoons grated cheese, 3 cloves of garlic, 1 tablespoon tomato paste, salt, pepper, nutmeg.

Halve the aubergines horizontally, and soak for 1/2 an hour in salted water. Now parboil them for 15 minutes, drain them, let them cool down, and scoop out some of their inner flesh. In the meantime start preparing the stuffing by frying the chopped onion in olive oil. To this add the minced meat. When this has browned, put in some of the scooped-out aubergine flesh. Now pour in the tomato paste mixed with some warm water. When the sauce has reduced somewhat, remove from the fire and allow to cool slightly. Now stir in the eggs and the cheese. Season with a pinch of grated nutmeg. Use this tasty meat sauce to stuff the aubergine halves.
Peel the potatoes and slice them rather thickly. Layer them on the bottom of an oiled oven dish, and season with salt, freshly ground black pepper, and the chopped garlic. Place the stuffed aubergines on top of the bed of potatoes. Bake in a medium oven till the potatoes are ready. In case the aubergines get done before the potatoes, remove them from the oven. The aubergines can be substituted with large marrows, or else you can use both marrows and aubergines.

Qara' baghli mimli fil-brodu
Stuffed marrows cooked in broth

1/2 kilo beef or pork mince, 1 kilo large marrows, 1 small finely chopped onion, 2 chopped bacon rashers, 2 beaten eggs, a heaped tablespoon of grated cheese, a small bunch of chopped parsley, salt, pepper, crushed coriander seeds.

For this recipe, the vegetables are left whole. Cut a lid off the top of each marrow, and using a teaspoon scoop out as much flesh as possible from the raw marrows. Prepare the stuffing using the above ingredients mixed with some of the scooped out marrow flesh. Fill the marrows with this mixture, and dust the open ends with flour to seal, and prevent the meat from falling out during cooking. Now make a broth using some marrow bones and root vegetables (a kohl rabi, a carrot, an onion), and simmer the marrows for about 40 minutes in this broth to which they will impart a most delectable flavour. You can also boil potatoes in the soup which are then served with the marrows as a main dish.

QARA' TWIL MIMLI
STUFFED LONG MARROW OR GOURD

The long marrow comes into season around early June and lasts till October. These marrows are like very large bananas, with a diameter of about 8cm. They can reach a length of 60cm. The colour of this vegetable can be described as being a pastel green hue. The outer skin has to be scraped off, whilst much of the inside is inedible and is discarded. Each long marrow has to be cut into sections of about 10cm in length, and the inside scooped out with a knife before stuffing. It is only the 1/2cm or so of the outer flesh which is eaten. This part of the vegetable is also used for making candied peel.

To cook stuffed long marrow, follow the recipe as for stuffed marrows above, but substituting the inside flesh with extra minced meat.

Sauce which can be served with stuffed marrows:-
Fry 3 cloves of crushed garlic in olive oil. Add 1/2 dozen peeled and chopped tomatoes. Cook for a few minutes, and add the stuffed marrows. Cover and simmer very gently for several minutes before serving.

FRITTURI TAL-QARA' BAGHLI MIMLI
STUFFED MARROW FRITTERS

This is an ideal way of using up any left-overs from the two preceding recipes. You cut the previously cooked marrows or long marrows into rings about 1.5cm thick, dust them with flour and turn them in some beaten egg flavoured with chopped garlic and parsley, then you fry them in hot oil. Serve with tomato sauce.

QARA' BAGHLI BIZ-ZALZA PIKKANTI
VEGETABLE MARROWS WITH PIQUANT SAUCE

1 kilo vegetable marrows washed and cut into 1/2cm thick slices. For piquant sauce recipe, see page 72. Fry the marrow slices on both sides in plenty of oil until golden and tender. Drain the slices, and place them in a deep pyrex dish. Pour the piquant sauce over them, and serve cold as an accompaniment to meat or fish, or as a light supper.

FRITTURI TAL-HAXIX
VEGETABLE FRITTERS

In Malta *fritturi* or fritters are commonly made with boiled vegetable left overs, such as kohl rabi, marrows, gourds, and even lettuce or endive. The cooked vegetables are cut up or left whole according to taste, and dusted with flour. Then they are dipped into beaten egg which has been seasoned with chopped parsley and garlic, and fried in oil or butter. The resulting crispy fritters are served with a squeeze of lemon, usually as an accompaniment to a main dish of meat. A welcome change to plain salads and boiled vegetables.

FRITTURI TAL-FJUR TAL-QARA' BAGHLI
MARROW FLOWER FRITTERS

Even the delicate orange-yellow coloured flowers of the vegetable marrow (*qara' baghli*) are made into fritters and considered a delicacy! You must make a thickish batter with flour, water and a pinch of baking powder. Mix a beaten egg into this and season well. Rinse the brightly coloured flowers, cut off the tougher parts of the stalks, dip into the batter and fry in oil or butter. Serve with lemon wedges.

Forma tal-Bringiel
Aubergine Pudding

An unusual and most delicious way of cooking aubergines when they are in season.

2 aubergines, 60g grated parmesan, 3 beaten eggs, 6 tomatoes, 2 cloves of garlic, a few basil leaves.

Peel, slice and soak 2 aubergines in salted water for 1/2 an hour. Drain them, fry in olive oil, and drain again. Meanwhile make a basil and garlic flavoured tomato sauce . Butter a pudding basin, and layer this with the tomato sauce, the sliced aubergines, the grated cheese and the beaten eggs till the basin is 3/4 full. Seal with grease-proof paper and tie up with string; place the pudding basin in a large pan half full with water, put on the fire, and cook for about 1 hour or till the eggs set. Now turn the pudding out of the basin, cut into thick slices, and serve hot or cold, accompanied by more tomato sauce, if liked, and grated cheese.

Insalata tas-sustanza
A cooked vegetable salad

This cooked salad goes down well with all types of fish, and is equally good on its own as a vegetarian dish.

1/2 kilo marrows, 1/2 kilo string beans, 2 onions, 4 or 5 potatoes, tomato puree, olive oil, marjoram and garlic.

Pour some olive oil into a saucepan. Layer the vegetables, starting with the sliced onion, then the beans, the potato slices seasoned with chopped garlic, and finally the thickly sliced marrows. Season with salt, pepper, and a lot of marjoram. Sprinkle with olive oil, and pour in 1/2 a cupful of water into which you have stirred a dessertspoon of tomato paste. Cover the saucepan tightly, and bring to the boil. Lower heat and simmer very gently for about one hour. This dish is also very good eaten cold.

KAPUNATA
GREEN PEPPER AND AUBERGINE SALAD

A delicious summertime vegetable dish - excellent both warm and cold, on its own or as an accompaniment to fried fish.

2 aubergines, 6 green peppers, 6 tomatoes, 2 onions, 4 cloves of garlic, 6 olives, marjoram, 1 tablespoon of capers, a dozen fresh basil leaves.

Slice the onions and fry in oil, adding the diced aubergines, the deseeded green-peppers, the peeled and chopped tomatoes, and the crushed garlic. Season with salt and pepper. Cover, and allow to stew slowly till the peppers are soft. When they are done, add the stoned and chopped olives, the capers, and the herbs. Stir and remove from the fire. *Kapunata* will keep several days in the fridge.

TADAM MIMLI
STUFFED TOMATOES

1 tomato per person, 2 cups of breadcrumbs, a tablespoon of capers, 6 stoned black olives, 2 cloves of crushed garlic, fresh herbs to taste - marjoram, mint, basil and parsley, sea-salt, black pepper, olive oil.

Make a stuffing by mixing the breadcrumbs, olives, capers, garlic, herbs and seasoning. Bind with some olive oil. Halve the tomatoes horizontally and scoop out the seeds and some of their inner flesh. Now fill the tomatoes with the stuffing; they do not have to be too tightly packed, and it does not matter if some of the filling actually spills over. Tomatoes stuffed in this way are a most delectable and refreshing summertime dish. They can be eaten on their own, or as an accompaniment to fish. If you like, you can sprinkle the tomatoes with a little olive oil, place them in an oven dish and bake them for half an hour in a medium oven.

BARBULJATA
TOMATO AND EGG SCRAMBLE

2 cloves of garlic, 3 large tomatoes, 8 eggs.

Fry the crushed garlic in olive oil, add the peeled and chopped tomatoes and cook gently for a few minutes. In the meantime beat the eggs lightly, add them to the pan, season with sea-salt and a pinch of black peppper and stir occasionally with a wooden spoon. Since the tomatoes give off a lot of liquid, the eggs will not solidify so easily as with some omelettes. Actually *barbuljata* should always be a bit runny and creamy. This is an ideal summertime supper dish.

BZAR AHDAR MIMLI BL-INCOVA
STUFFED GREEN PEPPERS WITH ANCHOVY

4 large green peppers, 2 cups of breadcrumbs, 1 tablespoon capers, 8 olives, a bunch of parsley, mint leaves, 8 fillets salted anchovy, olive oil, freshly milled pepper.

Choose fresh, shiny peppers; remove their stalks and seeds, and wash them well. Chop the anchovy fillets; stone and cut up the olives, and mix together with the breadcrumbs, the capers, the crushed mint and chopped parsley. Season with pepper, and bind with a little olive oil. Fill each pepper with this mixture and fry them in the oil, turning occasionally until golden brown all over. When the peppers are done, remove from the oil and serve hot or cold.

BZAR AHDAR MIMLI BIL-LAHAM
GREEN PEPPERS WITH MEAT AND RICE STUFFING

6 green-peppers, cleaned and washed as in preceding recipe.
For the filling: 300g mince (beef,pork or mixed), 1 rasher bacon, 3 tablespoons raw rice, 1 large onion, 1 tablespoon tomato paste, 1 egg, 1 tablespoon grated cheese.

Fry the chopped onion in oil, add the minced meat, and the slightly diluted tomato paste. Cook for a couple of minutes only. Now stir in the rice, the grated cheese, a beaten egg, and the seasoning. Fill the peppers with this stuffing; first fry them in olive oil until brown all over, then remove and transfer them to a casserole dish in which you have prepared a plain tomato sauce, and finally stew them gently for about 25 minutes.

HOBZ BIZ-ZEJT U TADAM
BREAD WITH OIL AND TOMATOES

Malta's most popular summertime snack. Cut thick slices of crusty fresh bread - the genuine Maltese loaf is of course ideal for this dish. Halve a tomato and rub it into the surface of the bread slices, so that they acquire a nice reddish hue. The best tomatoes are the really juicy summer tomatoes. Pour some olive oil onto a plate, and dip the bread slices into the oil, sprinkle liberally with black pepper, coarse sea-salt, and according to preference, any of the following ingredients: olive slices, capers, chopped raw onion, herbs, mostly marjoram and mint leaves, boiled butter beans, crispy lettuce, pickled vegetables - also known in Malta as *gardiniera* - and anchovy fillets or chunks of tinned tuna fish. There is really no fixed rule as to what goes into one of these delicious sandwiches. I suppose it's just a question of taste or of what one has been brought up on.

FUL TAN-NANNA
GRANNY'S BROAD BEANS

1 1/2 kilo broad bean pods, a thick slice of white bread, 3 large cloves of chopped garlic, vinegar, olive oil, a large bunch of parsley, pepper and salt.

Remove the beans from their pods, and cut off the nail shaped bit on top of each bean. Place the beans in a saucepan, and cover just with water. Bring to the boil, and allow to simmer till the beans are done. In the meantime having soaked the bread in some vinegar, squeeze this out, chop the bread coarsely and add it to the drained beans, together with the garlic and finely chopped parsley. Season to taste, mix well, and sprinkle with olive oil. Return to the fire for a further 3 minutes. This dish can be eaten as an accompaniment to fish or meat, or served as a supper dish with eggs.

Maltese idiom: Fula f'qara'.
Translation: A broad bean in a pumpkin; meaning, a very rare occurrence or something impossible.

FUL IMGIDDEM
BITTEN BEANS

Another recipe for these nutritious beans, is best made towards the end of the season, when the *ful* are very big.

1 kilo beans, 1 large onion, 1 tablespoon tomato paste, a bunch of fresh mint, olive oil, a thick slice of white bread soaked in vinegar, seasoning.

Prepare the beans as in the previous recipe and then soak in water. In the meantime chop the onion, and sautee for 10 minutes. Stir in the tomato paste mixed with a tumbler of water. Cook a few minutes further, and then add the beans and enough water just to cover them. When the beans are done, add the bread, which you have squeezed dry of the vinegar, the mint leaves, and the seasoning. The bread will absorb the little remaining liquid, and you will be left with a most tasty dish.

QLUB TAL-QAQOCC LA TORKA
ARTICHOKE HEARTS, TURKISH STYLE

Napoleon Bonaparte, during his short visit to Malta towards the end of the 18th century, officially abolished slavery. Up to that time it was common for upper class families to keep slaves, some of which would have been Turks.

1/2 a dozen artichoke hearts, garlic, parsley, 1 lemon, 2 teaspoons of cornflour.

Strip the artichokes of their outer leaves, remove the chokes and halve the hearts. Rub the hearts with a halved lemon, place them in a saucepan, and cover just with water. Season the water with salt and a squeeze of lemon. Cook slowly till the hearts are tender, and pour off half of the remaining water. Dilute the cornflour with cold water, stir into the saucepan, and cook a further 5 minutes. At the same time sprinkle the hearts with olive oil, lots of chopped parsley, chopped garlic to taste, and freshly ground black pepper.

FAZOLA BAJDA
SALAD WITH BUTTER BEANS

Nowadays, little plates of beans cooked this way are served in the bars with drinks in order to attract custom. They are very appetizing indeed, and a few of these beans make an ideal filling for *hobz biz-zejt* (page 37).

1/2 kilo dried haricot beans, 4 cloves crushed garlic, a large bunch of chopped parsley, olive oil, a few drops of tabasco, seasoning.

Soak the beans overnight in plenty of water. Change the water and boil till the beans are done but not overcooked. Drain the beans and allow them to cool. Season with coarse sea-salt, freshly milled black pepper, the garlic, lots of chopped parsley, and the tabasco. Pour in some good olive oil, mix well and serve.

FORMA TAL-PIZELLI
PEA PUDDING

500g shelled peas, 200g pork belly, 100g mixed chicken liver and giblets, 2 onions, 2 eggs, 2 egg yolks, a pinch of thyme, butter, seasoning.

Sautee the finely chopped onions in plenty of butter. Add the diced pork and chopped giblets, brown all over, cover the pan, and allow to cook slowly. In the meantime boil the peas for a few minutes in salted water, drain them, and pass them through a sieve or puree them in an electric blender. Beat the whole eggs with the egg yolks, and stir them into the pea puree, together with about 1/3 of the meat sauce. Season the mixture well with salt, pepper and thyme, and pour into a buttered pudding basin. Place this in a hot but not boiling waterbath (up to 3/4 of the way up in water), and cook slowly for 1 to 2 hours till a knife comes out clean. Let the pudding cool down, and carefully turn out on to a wide dish. Cut into thick slices and serve accompanied with the rest of the meat sauce.

Zebbug mimli
Stuffed olives

Both Malta and Gozo have a town called Zebbug, which means olives or olive trees. It is to be assumed that olive trees once thrived on these islands. Certain archeological finds testify to a considerable olive oil industry during Roman times. Much of the beautiful antique Maltese furniture was manufactured from olive wood.

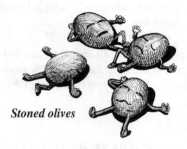

Stoned olives

30 largish, stoned, green olives, crumbs from 4 slices of dry white bread, 6 cleaned and chopped salted-anchovy fillets, 1-2 teaspoons capers, 3 crushed and chopped cloves of garlic, chopped herbs (basil, marjoram) to taste, a pinch of black pepper, some olive oil. Make a forcemeat out of all the ingredients except the whole olives, binding with the olive oil. Patiently fill the olives with this stuffing. Stuffed olives are ideal to have with cocktails, and are always served at weddings and other occasions. Stuffed olives can also be dipped into a light batter and deep fried.

Pulpetti tal-pastard
Cauliflower fritters

1/2 boiled cauliflower, 6 boiled potatoes, 2/3 garlic cloves, small bunch of parsley, 1 beaten egg, seasoning.

These fritters are usually made whenever there is any cauliflower left over from some other dish. Mash the potatoes together with the cauliflower in a bowl. Add the chopped garlic and parsley, and season to taste. Mix in the beaten egg. Using a large tablespoon, scoop out the mixture and fry in hot oil. The mixture should be rather runny. These fritters can be served hot or cold, with a twist of lemon.

BIGILLA
SPICY BEAN PASTE

There was a time when vendors used to come to the villages with their horse-drawn carts selling hot *bigilla*. These are now very rare, probably an extinct species.

1/2 kilo dried broad beans, 1/2 cup olive oil, 1 lemon, 1 small hot red pepper, 8 cloves of garlic, a handful of parsley, some fresh mint leaves and marjoram, salt.

Soak the broad beans for 24 hours, changing water at least 3 times. Cook the beans in fresh but little water for 1 1/2 hours. Drain off any excess liquid. Mash and liquidize the beans adding the olive oil, the juice of the lemon, the crushed hot red pepper, the crushed and chopped garlic, the finely chopped parsley, the herbs, and the salt. This puree can now be served (hot or cold) either as a snack, on fresh bread which is first spread with tomato puree or ideally, as a dip. If you like it really hot, make some *felfel*, by mixing oil with crushed hot peppers, and pour some of this oil over your *bigilla*.

STUFFAT TAL-PASTARD
CAULIFLOWER STEW

1 small or half a large cauliflower, a handful of raisins, 6 potatoes, 6 olives, 2 large sliced onions, a small bunch each of marjoram and mint. Optional: 1 tin of tuna fish.

Brown the onions in a pan with plenty of olive oil; pour in a tablespoon of tomato paste diluted with a little warm water, stir and let simmer for 10 minutes. Season with plenty of marjoram and mint. Add the potatoes, cover with water, and season with salt and a little pepper. Let the potatoes cook a while, then add the cauliflower florets, the olives, and the raisins. Simmer till the cauliflower is tender. This dish is also good cold.

If you are not a vegetarian, you can enhance this dish by adding some fish fillets to the stew some 15 minutes before the end of cooking time. If fresh fish is not available, tinned tuna fish goes very well with this dish, in which case you add it at the very end.

42

Stuffat tal-Qaqocc bil-Ful u Pizelli
Artichoke Stew with Beans and Peas

A delicious vegetarian dish which was very popular in our family at Easter time.

8 artichokes, 1/2 a kilo broad beans, 1/4 kilo peas, 2 onions, 1 lemon.
Strip the artichokes from their outer leaves, cut the hearts in half, and remove the chokes. Rub them with lemon and place in a bowl with water. Peel the beans and shell the peas. Slice the onions and fry in olive oil. Add a tablespoon of tomato paste with a little water, and bring to the boil. Now add all the vegetables and a little more water if neccessary. Season with salt and pepper, and cook slowly till the artichokes are done.

Qaqocc mimli
Stuffed Artichokes

4 whole artichokes, breadcrumbs made from 2 slices of dry bread, 2 black olives, 4 cloves of garlic, a bunch of parsley, seasoning, olive oil, vinegar.

This dish is ideal at the beginning of the artichoke season, when the leaves are still rather tender. The younger the artichokes, the better, though of course, the more expensive. Soak the artichokes for half an hour in salted water. In the meantime prepare the stuffing with the breadcrumbs, the garlic, olives and parsley - all finely chopped, salt, freshly milled black pepper, and olive oil to bind. Knock the artichokes against the kitchen table, and part their leaves. Stuff the bread mixture between the leaves, and place the artichokes upright, side by side, in a saucepan. Pour in water up to half the height of the artichokes, add a tablespoon of vinegar and some salt, and sprinkle with olive oil. Cover tightly, bring to a slow boil, then reduce to a simmer; when the leaves are easily removed, the artichokes are ready for eating. Take the artichokes out of the water, and allow them to cool. Usually artichokes are eaten by detaching the leaves one by one, and scraping off the edible parts by pulling each leaf between the upper and lower front teeth! When all the leaves have been eaten and discarded, you are left with the heart, which should be eaten with a little olive oil or a suitable dressing.

43

PITRAVI
BEETROOT PICKLE

1.5 kilos beetroots, 150g sugar, 3/4 litre brown vinegar, a few cloves, a 3cm stick of cinnamon.

Wash and scrub the beetroots very well, and boil until tender. Allow them to cool and remove their skin. Boil up the vinegar with the sugar and whole spices, stirring constantly until the sugar dissolves. Leave to cool, and pour over the halved beetroots in sterilized jars. Beetroots pickled in this way will keep for many months and will add a nice spicy tang to any salad.

QXUR TAD-DULLIEH
PICKLED WATER-MELON RIND

The succulent red flesh of the water-melon is extremely refreshing during the hot summer months, when this fruit is so abundant, but it is a pity to discard the rind when it can be turned into such a delicious sweet pickle.

500g melon rind, 125g salt dissolved in 1 litre of water, 1/2 litre white vinegar, 2 cups of water, 500g sugar, 1 stick of cinnamon, 6 whole cloves.

Peel the melon as thinly as possible. Cut up the rind into 1cm wide strips and immerse them in the salted water. Bring to the boil and simmer for half an hour. Change the water and repeat with fresh, unsalted water, simmering for a further 10 minutes.
Change the water again and keep simmering until the rind is tender. Allow to cool, and leave untouched overnight. Now mix the vinegar, water and sugar with the whole spices and heat until the sugar is dissolved. Insert the drained melon rind and simmer for about 1 1/2 hours. The syrup will thicken, and the rind become translucent. Pour into sterilized jars and seal. This pickle will keep for about a year. It is very good as an accompaniment to cold cuts and with ham sandwiches.

Maltese saying: Ghajnejh ikbar min zaqqu.
Translation: He thinks his stomach can hold what his eyes behold; meaning, he is a glutton.

MEAT DISHES

A visit to the butcher takes place about twice a week, or, in these days of fridges and freezers only once. A butcher's shop in Malta is usually a small place, and you will not see such a variety of already cut and trimmed meats as is common in most European countries. Instead, more likely, there will be larger pieces, such as whole shoulders or legs, hanging down from large hooks, and the butcher will cut from these according to order. This can have its advantage, since the housewife will ask the butcher to cut the meat exactly as she wants it and according to the dish she is going to prepare. Thus she will ask for mince to make stuffing, for thin slices of frozen beef (most of our beef is imported) for *bragoli*. She will ask him to cut off that nice looking piece for roasting on Sunday, and that bit for making a broth, and some marrow bones of course, which she'll get free!

Unlike Italy and France, we do not boast of a large assortment of cured meats, salamis, and pates. On the contrary, there is only one type of sausage worthy of the name *zalzett Malti* - literally, Maltese sausage. It is made of pork meat and fat and spiced with garlic, parsley, peppercorns and coriander seeds. It can be eaten raw, fried, grilled or boiled. Those of you who like this sort of thing, get some, or ask the hotel receptionist to get you some from a reputable butcher. For those who have the guts (please excuse the pun) there is a recipe in this book for traditional Maltese sausage. It's quite easy to make, but requires a bit of patience and half a morning's hard work unless you have a sausage-making machine.

By tradition, meat is not eaten on Fridays, and many Maltese families have now adopted the English custom of roast - whether it is pork, beef or mutton - on Sundays, and I think I'll start off this section with this recipe.

Maltese saying: il-baqra kolla tinbieh.
Translation: Every part of the cow will sell.

45

Patata l-forn
Baked potatoes

Don't think I made a mistake and put a vegetarian dish in the meat chapter! Many Maltese call their dish of roast meat, *patata l-forn*, which means, literally, roast potatoes. This is probably because the joint is always surrounded by so many halved potatoes, which acquire such a lovely crust, after some time in the oven. Or else maybe it's the taste of crushed aniseed with which the potatoes are spiced, combined with the juices of the meat, which penetrate the crispy potatoes, which make them even more desirable to eat than the meat itself!
Choose large potatoes for this dish, not new potatoes, 1 or 2 per portion, depending on their size. Peel them and halve them or slice rather thickly. Pour 2 tablespoons of good quality vegetable or olive oil into an oven dish big enough to take the potatoes and the meat, and place this in a preheated oven for about 10 minutes. Now put the potato halves into the dish, tossing them around in the oil so that they get coated all over. Some sliced onions can also be added with the potatoes. Sprinkle the potatoes quite liberally with sea-salt, black pepper and whole aniseed. If you think the potatoes will take longer to cook than your joint, give them a bit of a pre-roast, and then take them out again, and add the meat. For all types of meat rub with salt and black pepper and insert a couple of cloves of garlic into the meat. If cooking pork, rub the pork with slightly crushed or whole coriander seeds, and if cooking lamb, use rosemary instead. Roast in a moderate oven till the potatoes are crunchy brown, and enough juice has come out of the meat to be cooked as you like it.

Buljut
Boiled meat

You can use almost any type of beef for this recipe, but ideally meat which is neither suitable for grilling nor frying. The very slow cooking process will see to it that otherwise tough meat will become quite succulent and tender. The meat is cooked as in the recipe for meat broth (page 9), and then eaten warm or cold, with a green sauce made in the following way:-
Soak a thick slice of white bread in some brown vinegar. After a few minutes, squeeze out the vinegar and chop the bread finely together with 2 or 3 cloves of crushed garlic. To this add lots of chopped parsley, salt and freshly milled black pepper. Now pour in 3 tablespoons of olive oil, in a trickle, stirring continuously and thoroughly. A few chopped capers do enhance this sauce, as does a small chopped red pepper, if you like it hot!
Buljut is usually served with steamed potatoes, and vegetables which have been sprinkled with coarse sea-salt and crushed aniseed.

46

ZALZETT MALTI
MALTESE SAUSAGE

Maltese sausages are made with pork which can be minced or chopped. The ratio of meat to fat should be about 4 to 1.

For each kilo of meat you need: 4 cloves of garlic coarsely chopped, a tablespoon each of whole coriander seeds and black peppercorns, a teaspoon of salt, a cup of chopped parsley.

Get your butcher to keep some intestines for the casings.
Once you get down to sausage making, it's not really worth the hassle unless you intend making a large quantity. After having minced or chopped the meat, mix it well with the rest of the ingredients. Wash the intestines thoroughly under running water. Most modern food processors have a sausage-making attachment. If not, stuffing the casings by hand can be quite a laborious process and takes some getting used to. If you intend eating the sausages soon, hang them in an airy place for a couple of days. Otherwise, the sausages can be kept in the freezer until required. Hung sausages are good raw, with fresh bread and butter, but frozen sausages must be cooked, either poached with a bay leaf, fried, or grilled. See next recipe.

47

Stuffat Tal-Zalzett
Hot-pot with Maltese sausage

This delicious stew is made using Maltese sausage, or any similiar type of pork sausage.

1/2 kilo peeled and halved potatoes, 2 large, thickly sliced onions, 3 thickly sliced carrots, 1 small quartered cabbage, caraway seeds, seasoning, 1 glass white wine, 4-6 Maltese sausages. If such sausages are not available, you can cook this stew using pork chops instead, substituting 1 chop for each sausage.

Pour a little olive oil into a casserole. Now layer the casserole first with the onions, then with the potatoes seasoned with salt, pepper, and some crushed caraway seeds, the carrots, the sausages (which you must prick), or pork chops if preferred, and finally the cabbage. Pour in a glass of water or white wine, bring to bubbling point, lower the heat, and allow to simmer very gently for about 40 minutes. The fat from the sausages will melt to the bottom of the pan, and combined with the wine, will make a very tasty gravy. If using pork chops make sure they have quite a bit of fat on. Before anyone has time to say *cholesterol,* remember this is a real cookery book and not a health-food guide. My grandmother used to love eating bread spread with pork dripping. She lived to the ripe old age of 99!

Maltese honey sold in whisky bottles

Maltese housewife with a freshly baked *timpana* (page 18)

Ingredients for *bigilla* (page 41)

Gbejniet (page 7) and reed baskets in which they are made

At the fish market - swordfish

Scorpion fish for *aljotta* (page 14)

Pumpkins ripening under a clear Maltese sky

Prickly pears (page 91)

Rabbit - shaped *figolla* (page 86)

Flowers of the vegetable marrow (page 33)

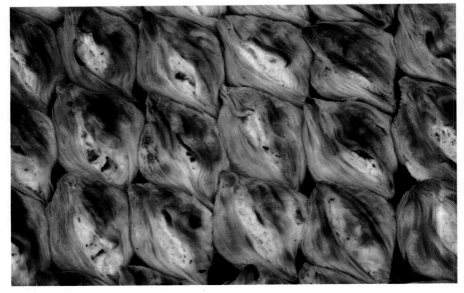

Pastizzi (page 26)

Mqaret (page 85)

Lampuki

Maltese capers taste best

Qubbajt (page 90)

Snail stew (page 64)

FRIKASSIJA TAL-HARUF
LAMB STEW

Ideally you would require the shoulder or ribs and offal (liver, kidneys) of a young, fresh lamb. If fresh lamb is not available, however, frozen lamb chops are a good substitute for this dish.

1 1/2 kilos lamb, 2 onions, 2 cups of peas, a bunch of parsley, butter, 1 lemon.

Cut the lamb into chunks. Slice the onions not too thinly, place them in a saucepan together with the pieces of lamb, and season with salt, black pepper, and a hint of lemon zest. Barely cover with water, add a large knob of good butter, and simmer very gently - making sure that the water never actually boils - until the meat is cooked. If you are using fresh lamb, this will become flaky, it will slip off the bone very easily and it will melt in your mouth. Finally throw in the peas and the finely chopped parsley. Cook for a further 5 minutes. Serve on a bed of rice accompanied by lemon wedges.

HARUF BIZ-ZALZA TAL-KAPPAR
LAMB OR MUTTON WITH CAPER SAUCE

What a wonderful way of using up the leftovers of a leg or shoulder of roast mutton.

Leftovers of roast mutton or lamb, 1 cup of barley, 1 carrot, 1 onion, 1 kohl rabi, 2 tablespoons of capers, vinegar, white sauce (*bechamel*).

Soak the barley overnight in water. Place the mutton, bone and all, in a pot with the whole or halved vegetables and the barley.
Cover with water, bring to the boil, and simmer slowly till the barley is cooked but not overdone. You now have a delicious barley soup, which can be eaten as a first course. Take the meat out of the soup, and remove any morsels which are still attached to the bone; discard the bone.
In the meantime prepare a plain white (*bechamel*) sauce, according to your favourite recipe. While this is still on the fire, add the capers, roughly chopped, and a teaspoon of vinegar. Into this mix the bits of mutton or lamb, which should by now be very tender, and serve immediately. If you live in a Northern country, and capers are hard to come by, you can substitute with fresh, chopped dill. I have recently discovered that this recipe is also ideal for left-over roast chicken or turkey.

Bragoli
Beef olives

Why this dish is referred to as such by the English is beyond me. I suppose the rolled and stuffed slices of beef very remotely resemble olives. This is a dish which seems to be popular in many European countries. Even in Malta there are several versions, of which I'm giving my favourite.

1 kilo of topside of beef cut into 12 thin slices, 2 onions, 1 carrot, 5 slices of crustless white bread, 3 sliced hard-boiled eggs, 6 rashers of bacon, chopped parsley, 2 cloves of garlic, 2 bay leaves, black pepper freshly ground, salt.

Beat each of the meat slices flat with a kitchen hammer and spread them out on the table top. Grind the bread to crumbs. Prepare a stuffing by mixing the breadcrumbs with the chopped bacon, the garlic, the parsley, and the seasoning. Heap a tablespoon or two of the stuffing onto each beef slice, and top with a slice or segment of egg.

Roll the meat slices lengthwise over the stuffing, and tie up with thread, or keep together with wooden toothpicks.

Pour some oil or melt some lard in a large pan, and brown the beef olives all over in this, together with the bay leaves. You'll probably have to do this in two rounds. Transfer the browned *bragoli* to a casserole. In the same oil or fat, fry the sliced onions and carrot. Pour 1/2 a glass of robust red wine over the frying onions, let it bubble and then pour this sauce over the beef olives in the casserole. Now stew slowly for 1 1/2 hours. At some stage you might have to add a little stock or water, but not too much, otherwise the *bragoli* will boil and not stew. When the *bragoli* are ready, remove the thread or toothpicks, and serve with peas and mashed potatoes. The sauce will be very tasty.

Bragolun
Giant beef-olive

Instead of making a lot of small beef-olives, it might be more convenient to make just one rather large one. This is an ideal substitute for *bragoli,* when you have a party with many guests.

1 kilo topside of beef cut into one piece, beaten and flattened into one large slice, stuffing as for previous recipe, a piece of caul.

Spread the breadcrumb mixture over the meat slice, roll it, wrap it in the caul, and secure it with string. Brown the *bragolun* all over and proceed to make the sauce and stew as in the recipe for *bragoli.* Remove the string, and cut into thickish slices before serving.

Laham fuq il-fwar
Meat on steam

This is an easy and excellent method for cooking beef which might be too tough for frying or grilling.

1/2 kilo rump steak cut into thinnish (1/4 cm) slices, the crumbs from 2 or 3 slices of dry bread, 2 chopped bacon rashers, 3 crushed cloves of garlic, parsley, butter, salt and pepper.

Mix thoroughly the breadcrumbs, the bacon and the garlic; season with parsley, sea-salt and black pepper from the mill. Now butter a small pyrex dish or a large soup plate and layer alternately with the meat slices and breadcrumb mixture. Add a tablespoon of water to the plate. Cover very tightly and steam over a simmering soup for about 1 hour.

Lucerto ibbuttunat
"Buttoned" silverside

1 whole cut of 1 kilo of silverside of beef, 12 small onions, 1 carrot, 2 rashers of streaky bacon, 2 cloves of garlic, some sprigs of parsley, a little thyme, red wine.

Pierce the meat at both ends twice or three times with a skewer. Stuff the holes with the bacon, the garlic and the parsley. Brown the meat all over in a large pan with oil or lard, then transfer it to a pot where it will fit comfortably. Now fry the onions and the chopped carrot in the same fat, and moisten with a glass of red wine. Stir, allow to bubble for a minute, and pour this sauce over the joint in the pot. Season with a pinch of thyme, and simmer for 2 hours. The meat will acquire the flavour of the wine, the bacon and the garlic, and you will get a very savoury sauce. The meat should be carved into thinnish slices. The slices will be decorated with pretty, pinkish, bacon "buttons". Any left-overs will also be delicious as cold cuts.

ILSIEN
TONGUE STEW

Cook the tongue or tongues as described in the recipe for broth with tongue on page 10. Now prepare a sauce. Fry 2 sliced onions in olive oil, add a tablespoon of tomato paste and a couple of peeled and quartered tomatoes, and stir-fry for a few minutes. Now ladle in about 1/4 of a litre of the broth, and insert the whole, skinned tongue or tongues, a chopped carrot, and a cupful of peas. Cook slowly till the carrots are slightly tender.

ILSIEN BIZ-ZALZA PIKKANTI
TONGUE WITH PIQUANT SAUCE

1 ox tongue, or 2 - 3 pork tongues, 2 sliced onions, 2 tomatoes peeled and chopped, 6 stoned black olives, a tablespoon of capers, a level teaspoon of granulated white sugar, a tablespoon of tomato puree and a glass of good red table wine.

Cook the tongues as described on page 10. Fry the onions in olive oil, stir in the tomato puree and the sugar. Pour in the table wine, add the olives, tomatoes and capers, and simmer the tongues in this sauce for 20 minutes. Serve with steamed potatoes.

Majjal Fgat
"Choked" Pork

When you are cooking a piece of pork leg or shoulder which is not large enough for a proper roast, you will find this an ideal and easy substitute recipe.

A cut of pork leg, preferably boneless, weighing between 500g and 700g, coriander seeds, 2 cloves of garlic, a bunch of parsley, some lemon rind, white wine, the crumbs from 3 slices of dry bread, salt, freshly milled pepper .

Brown the meat all over in a saucepan. Lay it on one side in the pan, and season the upper face with salt, pepper and crushed coriander seeds. Let it cook (or "choke") in its own juices very tightly covered for 1 hour. In the meantime prepare a mixture of breadcrumbs, lots of parsley, a pinch of grated lemon rind, and the chopped cloves of garlic. Spread this mixture on top of the joint, add a glass of dry white wine to the pan, and baste the meat with this. Leave for a further 1/2 hour or till the pork is properly cooked.

FALDA MIMLIJA
STUFFED FLANK

One whole piece of beef flank (about 1 kilo), 1/4 kilo minced pork, 1 chopped bacon rasher, 1 beaten egg, 1/2 a cup of breadcrumbs, 1 clove of garlic, 1 tablespoon grated cheese, chopped parsley, a few whole coriander seeds, pepper and salt.

Ask your butcher to cut a slit or pocket into your beef. Mix all the remaining ingredients together thoroughly, stuff the spicy mixture into the pocket and sew up the opening. The stuffed beef is now simmered very gently for about 2 hours in a broth with marrow bones and some root vegetables. Potatoes can be steamed over the pot. The meat is removed from the soup and cut into thickish slices and then served either with green sauce (page 46) or with a squeeze of lemon.

FRITTURI TAL-MOHH
BRAIN FRITTERS

In some Middle Eastern and North African countries, there are certain superstitions associated with the eating of brains - that the person who eats the brains will gain intelligence, or on the contrary, will become as stupid, as the animal from which the brains originally came. In Malta this superstition does not exist, so go ahead and eat as many brains as you like.

1 ox or 4 pigs' brains, flour, 2 eggs, a small bunch of parsley.

Soak the brains for 1 hour in salted water. Skin the brains, and steam them over a pot of boiling water or over a simmering soup, till just done. Cut the brains lengthwise into slices, and dip them lightly, first in flour, then into the well beaten eggs seasoned with the chopped parsley, salt and pepper. Melt some butter in a pan, and fry the brains on a very moderate fire, so the butter doesn't burn. Serve with lemon wedges.

Stuffat tal-Qlub tal-Qaqocc u Majjal
Pork and Artichoke-Heart Stew

Because of the tenderness and quality of the meat used in this recipe, and also because it is so easy to prepare, this is an ideal dish to cook for guests.

1/2 kilo pork tenderloin cut into thick rounds, half a dozen artichoke hearts washed and quartered, 1 large onion chopped finely, 1 cupful of peas, 1 tablespoon tomato paste.

Brown the pork slices in olive oil and put aside. In the same pan, fry the onion and the artichoke hearts, adding the tomato puree and a tumbler of water. Return the pork chunks to the pan, stir, and cook slowly till the hearts are tender. Towards the end of cooking time, add the peas.

Pulpettun
Meat roll

3/4 kilo minced pork, 1/4 kilo minced beef, 100g pork liver, 2 hard-boiled eggs, 3 raw eggs, a slice of ham, 1/2 a grated onion, chopped parsley, a few lightly crushed coriander seeds, a piece of caul, 1 large potato per person, seasoning.

Mix the minced meat in a bowl with the onion, the chopped ham, the parsley, the raw eggs, the coriander seeds and the seasoning.

Rinse the caul properly, squeeze it dry, lay it out flat on the table, and spread it with half of the meat mixture. On top of this place the roughly chopped pork liver and the whole hard-boiled eggs; cover with the rest of the meat mixture, and form into a Swiss-roll shape, wrapping the caul around it. If you find difficulty in obtaining caul, use cooking foil instead.

Cut the potatoes into thickish slices, place them on the bottom of an oiled or greased baking tray, season them well, and place the meat roll on top. Bake in a high oven for 1/4 of an hour, and then lower the heat to medium.

The meat loaf baked in caul will exude some delicious juices, which will also penetrate the potatoes. The *pulpettun* is now cut into slices about 1cm thick, and served with the baked potatoes.

Alternatively, you can boil the meat-roll in a pot of water with some root vegetables: a carrot, a kohl rabi, an onion, a stick of celery, and some potatoes. In this case, wrap the meat in a very thin sheet of muslin cloth instead of caul. You will also get a very tasty soup.

Any leftover slices of meat roll can be served cold with a crisp salad, or as sandwich fillers.

Pulpetti
Meat fritters

Whenever we children used to leave any scraps of meat on our plates, either because they were too tough, or had too much fat, father used to say: "You are spoilt; you don't know what it means to go hungry; you should have lived through the war - we never threw anything away then". Whenever there is a considerable amount of meat left over from a meal we keep it and then one or two days later we make these *pulpetti*.

1/2 a kilo cooked pork or beef, 4 large or 6 medium boiled potatoes, 1 egg, chopped parsley, seasoning, 1 onion, 1 tablespoon tomato puree.

Sautee the chopped onion in some olive oil or lard, add the tomato paste mixed with a glass of water, and cook for a further ten minutes to reduce the sauce. Mince the meat rather finely and mix it in a bowl together with the sauce, the parsley and the beaten egg. With floured hands, take lumps of the mixture and form into little balls or croquettes. Roll in flour, and fry in oil. The *pulpetti* can be eaten with salad or as an accompaniment to pasta with tomato sauce.

Flett tal-Majjal il-Forn
Stuffed pork fillet

2 pork fillets, 100g bacon, 50g breadcrumbs, 1 tablespoon of capers, 6 cloves of garlic, 4 stoned black olives, 10 potatoes, 2 onions, a pinch of thyme, a bunch of chopped parsley, seasoning.

Cut a slit, about 2cm deep, down the length of each of the fillets. Prepare a forcemeat with the breadcrumbs, the capers, the finely chopped olives, the crushed garlic and the herbs. Fill the pockets with this mixture, and sew them carefully together with white thread. Pour some olive oil into a large oven dish. Spread the onion and potato slices evenly on the bottom of the dish. Pour a glass of water over them, and season generously with sea-salt and freshly milled black pepper. Place the stuffed pork fillets on top of the potatoes and onions, and bake in a medium oven till the potatoes are ready. The pork will probably be cooked before the potatoes, in which case, remove the fillets from the oven, and wrap them up in cooking foil, or, alternatively, pre-bake the potatoes 25 minutes on a high fire before inserting the meat.
Cut the fillets into thickish slices and serve with the baked potatoes and onions. Don't forget to remove the thread.

FWIED MOQLI FIL-MINDIL
LIVER FRIED IN CAUL

1/2 kilo pork liver cut into slices, not too thick, bay leaves, a piece of caul, whole cloves of garlic, a lemon, sea-salt.

Sprinkle the slices of liver with the salt and allow to stand about half an hour. Rinse the caul under running water, squeeze it dry, and spread out on the kitchen table; now cut it into segments large enough to wrap the liver slices with. Place a bayleaf on to each piece of liver, wrap with the caul, and fry in oil or lard. Fry the whole cloves of garlic together with the liver, making sure they do not burn. When the liver is cooked, sprinkle with some lemon juice.

Maltese saying: Mejda tajba testment hazin.
Translation: A fat kitchen a lean will.

Chicken, Rabbit, Snails and Game

Tigiega Mimlija
Stuffed Chicken

1 medium sized roasting chicken or capon, 300g mixed pork and beef mince, a thick slice of bread soaked in milk, 75g bacon or ham in fine strips, 1/2 minced raw onion, 1 beaten egg, 1 hard-boiled egg in quarters, a little grated cheese, the chopped liver from the chicken, chopped parsley, a few lightly crushed coriander seeds, a small pinch of grated lemon rind, seasoning.

Squeeze the milk out of the bread, chop it up roughly and mix it with the mince and the rest of the ingredients for the stuffing. Season to taste with salt and black pepper. Loosen the skin over the breast of the bird with a sharp knife, and fill the space between the flesh and the skin with the stuffing. Sew up the opening with white thread. Now you can proceed in one of the two following ways, either:

1) Place the stuffed chicken in a large soup pot together with some root vegetables - a carrot, an onion, a kohl rabi and a stick of celery. Season, add a bay leaf, bring to the boil, and cook slowly till the chicken is ready. This method, will also give you an excellent soup.
or,
2) Line an oiled casserole dish with thick onion and potato slices, season well with crushed fennel seeds, ground black pepper and sea-salt. Pre-roast in a hot oven for some 25 minutes, add a little water to the dish, place the stuffed bird onto the bed of potatoes, lower the heat to medium and roast till you are satisfied that the chicken is cooked.

Frikassija tat-Tigieg
Chicken hot-pot

This is a very easy method for cooking chicken, which does not entail any frying or basting.

1 large chicken or 2 small ones (approximately 1.75 kilos in all), a large onion, 2 rashers of bacon or slices of cooked or smoked ham, 1 carrot, a handful of peas, a bunch of chopped parsley, a hint of lemon zest.

Cut the chicken up into pieces and place in a casserole dish or pot together with the giblets, the sliced onion and carrot and the chopped ham or bacon. Season with salt, pepper, and lemon zest. Pour in some water, but not enough to cover completely. Put the pot on a slow fire for about 1 hour, by which time the chicken should be cooked. Now add the peas, and cook a further five minutes. Finally add the chopped parsley. Serve on a bed of rice or with mashed potatoes.

Fenek moqli bit-tewm u nbid
Fried rabbit with garlic and wine

Of all the recipes for rabbit, this is definitely one of the best for bringing out the taste and goodness of a young fresh rabbit.

1 rabbit, 12 cloves of garlic, 2 bay leaves, 2 one-inch sticks of cinnamon, 4 cloves, allspice, salt and pepper, olive oil, red wine.

Joint the rabbit, season very well with sea-salt, coarsely crushed peppercorns and a hint of ground allspice. Fry in olive oil with the whole garlic cloves, the bay leaves, the cinnamon stick and the cloves. You should also fry the head, liver and lights. Whatever oil you use, it is important that it is not of an inferior quality, otherwise it may ruin the taste of the rabbit. Some cooks like to add a teaspoon of the commercial curry powder to the fried rabbit, omitting the whole spices altogether. Transfer the fried rabbit pieces with the spices to a larger saucepan in which you have about quarter of a bottle of robust red wine barely simmering on a very low flame. Cover well and stew the rabbit till the flesh easily comes off the bone. You can also put the pan in a low oven and cover with some aluminium foil. The rabbit will cook very nicely.

The Maltese like their rabbit served with chips, and of course lots of fresh bread to mop up the delicious juices!

Fenkata
Rabbit with Spaghetti

I found it difficult to translate the name for this dish. *Fenkata* is actually a glorification of the word *fenek*, which means rabbit - a feast or an orgy of rabbit almost.

Maltese people love to go out on summer evenings, in large groups either to celebrate some religious feast or political activity or just for the fun of it. They might hire a coach, and amidst much noise and colour, waving of flags, shouting and singing, travel to some village such as Mgarr or Bahrija, to have a *fenkata* - a real feast of spaghetti with rabbit sauce and pieces of fried rabbit, washed down with plenty of wine. On the 28th of June, the eve of the *Mnarja*, a midsummer folk's feast, thousands of people gather at the Gardens of Buskett, near the village of Dingli. There, the local farmers will be exhibiting the best of their produce: all types of vegetables, the best of the season's fruit, honey, carob syrup, wines, cheeses, livestock, pigeons, turkeys, and of course the Maltese's favourite, rabbits. Towards the end of the day there will also be some type of sportive competition such as horse racing. Then, as the glowing orange midsummer sun starts setting, stalls will be set up all around these beautiful gardens, serving fried rabbit, which would be slaughtered, chopped up and cooked on the spot! The aroma of the frying rabbit and garlic, mingled with the fresh country air and the scent of the pine and cypress trees, some of them centuries old, is absolutely heavenly. Hundreds of visitors will then, after a hearty meal, lay down on the earth beneath some tree and spend the warm night in these wonderful surroundings.

1 rabbit, a piece of pork belly weighing about 150g, 2 onions, 2 cloves of garlic, 1 bayleaf, 3 tablespoons of tomato paste or 12 peeled and chopped tomatoes, a handful of peas, a teaspoon of curry powder, lard or olive oil, seasoning.

Fry the diced onions, the whole garlic and the bay leaf in a deep pan in some hot lard or oil. Remove from the pan, and keep aside. In some more fat, brown the seasoned jointed rabbit (including the head and liver), and the piece of pork belly. Over these sprinkle a teaspoon of curry powder and add the tomato paste mixed with 2 tumblers of water, or the tomatoes. Return the fried onions, garlic and bayleaf. Cover tightly, and stew slowly till the rabbit is tender. 5 minutes from the end, add the peas. Now take out all the rabbit and pork pieces. Remove any edible morsels from the head of the rabbit, dice the pork, chop the liver roughly and return these to the sauce in the pan. This spicy sauce is eaten as a starter with boiled spaghetti, whilst the rabbit pieces are served as the main dish with potatoes.

GAMIEM
TURTLE DOVES

Game of this type is not usually available in the shops, though this is changing too, since birds such as quail and guinea-fowl are nowadays being bred in Malta. The average non-hunter family will only eat game if this is given to them by some hunter friend or neighbour.

2 birds per portion, about 100g pork sausage, 150g belly of pork, 2 sliced onions, 150g peas, 1 kohl rabi, 1 carrot, 1 onion, a stick of celery, 1/2 a bottle of red wine.

Having drawn and cleaned the birds properly, place them in a saucepan together with the whole vegetables, and cover with water. Simmer gently for about 1 1/2 hours till the birds are tender; remove the birds. Fry the sliced onions in olive oil in a separate, large pan; add the diced pork belly and pour in the wine. Fill the birds' cavities with the sausage meat and now add these too. After about 20 minutes, add the peas and simmer a further 10 minutes. Serve with mashed potatoes and slices of fried bread.

HAMIEM
AUNTIE LILY'S PIGEONS

This recipe was given to my mother by her sister, Lily. It is a marvellous way of cooking pigeons, which are now bred here, and also for any other type of smaller game birds or chicken.

2 birds per person, or if using small chickens, 1 chicken for every 2 portions, 1 lemon, rashers of bacon, a glass of good dry white wine, 1 tablespoon of brandy, 2 egg yolks, butter, a teaspoon of tarragon, seasoning.

Pluck, draw, and wipe the birds clean. Peel the lemon, retain the peel, and squeeze out the juice. Wrap 1 bacon rasher (2 for chickens) and a strip of lemon peel around each bird. Fry them gently in some good butter to brown all over. Pour in the cognac, set it alight and when the flame expires add the juice of the lemon, and the wine. Do not ruin this dish by using an inferior wine. Cover and cook slowly till the birds are done. The time will vary according to the size of the birds; wild game will take that much longer than birds which are bred. Now strain the pan juices into a pyrex bowl, stir in a tablespoon of good butter and the egg yolks. Place the bowl over a hot (but not boiling) water-bath and whisk continuously to produce a thickish sauce in the French fashion. Finally mix in the tarragon. Fresh tarragon is almost impossible to come by in Malta, but dry tarragon will do, otherwise omit altogether. Best served on a bed of saffron rice.

BEBBUX
SNAILS

On a fine day, after it has rained, you sometimes see people in fields or by the wayside, rummaging under stones and in the rubble walls. These people are probably searching for a type of land snail that is very common in Malta, and quite a delicacy too. Starved, live snails, can be found either at the Sunday market at Marsaxlokk, or at the women who sell herbs at Valletta Gate some mornings during the week. A bag of snails, enough for 2 to 4 portions doesn't cost more than 50 cents. Why not try smuggling some home with you in your luggage!

Method for cleaning snails:
Snails are usually starved for about 2 weeks before they are fit for eating. It is important however that the snails are still alive. Since the snails produce a lot of scum, they should be cleaned quite thoroughly.
Let the starved snails soak in plenty of salted water with vinegar (1/2 a glass) for about half an hour. Change the water and repeat the procedure. Now leave the snails for a few minutes under running water. Boil the snails in a large pot full of water. The snails are cooked when they are easily removed from their shells. With lots off patience, start extracting the snails out of their shells with a toothpick. Discard the shells. Some people actually prefer picking the snails out themselves, since they consider this to be part of the fun of eating snails. If this be the case, for any of the following recipes, the snails can be left in their shells

Bebbux bil-busbies
Snails with fennel

Snails, olive oil, butter, crushed garlic, 1 small red chilli, 2 teaspoons fennel seeds, a handful of chopped parsley, a tablespoon of brandy, 1 lemon, white wine, seasoning.

Clean the snails as described above.
Heat a tablespoon of olive oil and a knob of good butter in a pan. In this fry plenty of garlic (to taste), the finely chopped hot red chilli, and the crushed fennel seeds. Pour in the brandy, and allow to bubble till somewhat reduced. Now add the snails, the parsley, and half a glass of wine. Cover, simmer for a few minutes, remove from the flame, and squeeze some lemon juice over the snails. Serve hot or cold.

Bebbux bl-aljoli
Snails in garlic sauce

Snails, a cup of breadcrumbs, a bunch of parsley, 2 tablespoons olive oil, 8 cloves of garlic.

Clean the snails as described above.
Season the breadcrumbs with the crushed and finely chopped garlic, the finely chopped parsley, ground black pepper and salt. Moisten with the olive oil. Put a pan on a high fire; toss and roast the snails with the seasoned breadcrumbs for about 5 minutes. Bring piping hot to the table.

BEBBUX BIL-HWAWAR
SNAILS WITH SUMMER HERBS

Snails, 2 tablespoons olive oil, 1 hot red chilli, 1 onion, 4 cloves of garlic, 1 lemon, 2 small bunches each of mint and marjoram.

After cleaning the snails (as described in the method above, but without removing from their shells) cook them in water with one bunch of mint, one of marjoram, the quartered onion, and half the lemon. When the snails are ready, pour off the liquid and let them cool down. Now grind the leaves from the remaining marjoram and mint bunches together with the garlic and the chilli pepper in a mortar, at the same time pouring in the olive oil to make a paste. Toss the snails in this delectable herb-oil till they are coated all over.

Maltese proverb: Min ghandu il-bzar, iroxxu.
Translation: He who has the pepper shall season as he pleases.

65

Fish, octopus and everything
that comes from the sea

For much of the information contained in this chapter, I am grateful to my brother Michael, a keen diver and underwater explorer.

Every Maltese town and village is served by a fish vendor *(tal-hut)* who calls a couple of times a week to sell fish from the back of a van. In the smaller villages, he will park his van near the main square and wait patiently for customers, whilst in the larger towns he will move around from street to street, calling as he goes along *"ghadhom hajjin, ghadhom hajjin"*, - they're still alive! Earlier that morning, he would already have visited the main fish market in Valletta, or one of the fishing villages, St. Paul's Bay or Marsaxlokk. His fish will therefore always be fresh and varied according to the season. The housewife's choice of fish will be based on economics more than anything else. Tiny scorpion fish for *aljotta*, and baby mullet and bogue for deep frying are always cheap; octopus for stews and sauces, red mullet for stuffing and baking, and blue bream for grilling will cost that much more, but are favourites with the menfolk. And for really special occasions, there will be dentex, amberjack and grouper, the king of the deep. But who wants to pay Lm5 or Lm6 a kilo for dentex, when *lampuki* are selling at Lm1.50 and swordfish at Lm2.25?

Since many of my readers will be living hundreds of miles away from the Mediterranean, they should not hesitate to substitute with any other types of fish they may find in their particular region and that they think will be appropriate for the recipe. At Harrods in London I have seen lots of lovely very fresh Mediterranean fish, and I am sure that this is now available in many other parts of the United Kingdom too.

For the fish recipes, I have named those types of locally available fish, which in my opinion are most suited for each particular dish. In each case I have given the common English name, and the local name in brackets.

Maltese idiom: iz-zalza giet ghola mil-huta.
Translation: the sauce was dearer than the fish.

The tourist who asked the waiter if the fish was fresh or frozen.

RECIPE FOR GRILLED FISH - 1

The best type of fish for this recipe are saddled bream *(kahli)*, red mullet *(trill)*, gilt-head sea bream *(awrata)*, pandora *(pagell)*, horse-mackerel *(kavalli)*, and swordfish *(pixxispad)*.

For the stuffing:
Olive oil, 4 cloves of garlic, a cupful of breadcrumbs, 3 olives, 1/2 a tablespoon of capers, a few leaves of parsley and marjoram, seasoning, 1 lemon.

If using whole fish, first scale, clean and rinse the fish, leaving the head attached to the body, which always makes it more attractive when served on a plate. Rub the fish inside and out with garlic, salt, and ground pepper, and using a kitchen brush coat it with olive oil. Make a few gashes in the flesh of the fish, and into these insert garlic cloves and parsley. Make a stuffing with the breadcrumbs, the chopped olives, the capers, the marjoram and some seasoning. Bind with olive oil, and stuff the fish cavity with this mixture. Place the fish under a very hot grill. When the skin starts to peel off or to char, the fish is ready. Serve with lemon wedges.

If steakfish is used (such as swordfish or tunny), after coating with olive oil, spread the breadcrumb mixture on top of each slice of fish before grilling. A pretty way of decorating steak-fish grilled in this way, is with alternating stripes of finely chopped hard-boiled egg yolk and egg white.

RECIPE FOR GRILLED FISH - 2

100g butter, a teaspoon of crushed aniseed, a tablespoon of chopped capers, seasoning.

Clean and prepare the fish as in the first method. Blend the butter with the rest of the ingredients. Rub the fish inside and out with the spicy butter, and proceed to grill as described above.

Recipe for baked fish - 1

For this recipe use white bream *(sargu)*, sea-bass *(spnotta)*, blue-fin tuna *(tunacc)*, amberjack *(accjola)*, dolphin fish *(lampuka)* and pilot fish *(fanfru)*.

8 potatoes, 4 onions, 4 tomatoes, 6 tablespoons olive oil, 4 cloves of garlic, 8 black olives, seasoning, a large bunch of marjoram.

Cut the potatoes into 1.5cm slices, peel and quarter the onions and tomatoes. Blend the olive oil with the crushed garlic, the marjoram leaves and the seasoning. Pour this mixture into an ovenproof dish, and coat the potato slices with it by tossing them around in the dish. Now arrange the onion and tomato quarters around the border of the dish with the potato slices in the middle. On top of these put the whole olives. Bake in a high oven for 45 minutes or till the potatoes are only half cooked, then place the prepared fish beneath the layer of potatoes, so that the fish does not curl in the oven's intense heat; return the dish to the oven for a further 15 minutes. Now take the dish out again, and this time put the fish on top of the potatoes to get a nice crust, and bake for a final 5 minutes. At some stage it might be necessary to add a little hot water to the dish to prevent the potatoes from sticking.

70

Recipe for baked fish - 2

This recipe calls for a very thick slice of some large fish such as swordfish or tunny.

3/4 kilo swordfish in one piece, 2 large onions, 4/5 large potatoes, 4 tomatoes, 8 cloves of garlic, olive oil, whole black pepper, parsley, marjoram, oregano, bay leaves, seasoning.

Cut the peeled potatoes and onions into slices about 2cm thick, reserving 1 slice of onion for the fish stuffing. In your oven dish sprinkle the potato and onion slices with olive oil, some of the marjoram and oregano, black pepper, and salt. Coat them well, and roll the fish slice in this oil too. Pierce the fish in about four places close to the bone, then stuff the holes with the garlic, the rest of the herbs and some chopped onion. Place the bay leaf on top. Wrap the piece of fish in cooking foil, place in the centre of the dish, and cook in the oven on medium heat for 1 1/4 hours, then remove the fish from the foil, allowing its juices to mix with the potatoes, and the fish to brown slightly (15 minutes).

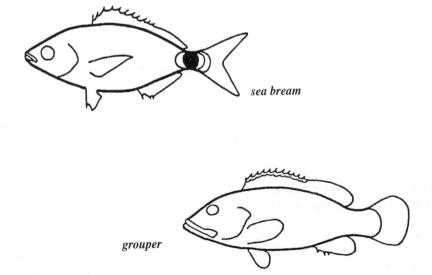

sea bream

grouper

Recipe for fried fish

Ideal for frying are swordfish, dolphin fish, bogue *(vopi)*, scad *(sawrell)*, garfish *(imsell)* and dogfish *(mazzola)*.

The smaller types of fish have to be scaled and cleaned properly and rinsed out in salted water. They are then left to drain in a colander with some coarse salt sprinkled over them. Larger fish are sliced into reasonably sized portions, either at home or by the fish vendor himself. Lampuki is also very good filleted, though most Maltese still prefer to cut it across the bone into sections of 8cm in length, the head, tail and fins usually kept to make soup. Fish steaks are also seasoned with salt, as with for smaller fish, and preferably allowed to stand for a couple of hours before frying. The fish are then dipped into flour and fried in hot oil. Very small fish are fried complete with head and tail, and allowed to get quite dark and crunchy in the boiling oil; the crispy tails are then eaten with much savour. *Mazzola* (dogfish) should be dipped into beaten egg before frying. The flesh of this fish is delicate and milky, so the outer coating of the egg batter makes a nice contrast. Fried fish is usually served with a sprinkling of lemon juice and a piquant caper sauce (below). *Insalata tas-sustanza* (page 34), and *kapunata* (page 35) are ideal vegetable dishes to accompany fried fish.

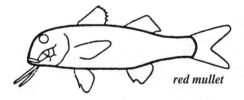

red mullet

Zalza pikkanti
Piquant sauce

4 cloves of garlic, 6 peeled tomatoes, 6 stoned black olives, 1 teaspoon capers, 1 tablespoon red-wine vinegar, 2 teaspoons salt, pepper, marjoram, olive oil.

Fry the whole garlic in hot oil, add the chopped tomatoes and allow to cook for a few minutes. Add the finely chopped olives, the marjoram leaves and whole capers; pour in the vinegar, stir well, season to taste and allow to simmer a further 10 minutes. Excellent with fried or grilled fish.

72

Recipe for Poached Fish

Fish which are ideal for poaching (this is not intended as a pun) are those types with a delicate flesh which would otherwise be ruined by grilling or frying, such as dentex *(denci)*, large-scaled scorpion fish *(cippulazz)*, gurnard *(gallina)*, meagre *(gurbell)*, and John Dory *(pixxi San Pietru)*. All these fish have a subtle taste which would easily be overpowered by the oils used in the grilling and frying processes. The fish must be scaled and cleaned, but left whole and not cut up into steaks. The cleaned fish is lowered into a fish kettle or similar vessel, and water is added, but only up to 3/4 of the way up. The water can be seasoned with some salt and fresh herbs (mint, marjoram). The fish is now poached on an extremely low flame, never actually boiling, until the flesh can be removed from the bone without much effort. The fish is now immediately lifted out of the water and allowed to cool down slightly; it is then served with a home-made mayonnaise or Maltese sauce (next recipe), and accompanied by the freshest and crispest of salads, olives, herbs, and small potatoes. The stock made in this way is the ideal base for an excellent *aljotta* (page 14).

73

Maltese Mayonnaise

There are two versions for this sauce, both of which go very well with poached fish.

(1) Make a mayonnaise according to your favourite recipe, using good olive oil and a clove of crushed garlic to flavour. Into this stir a tablespoon of the juice of a blood orange. Malta was once famous for these oranges which produce such an intense red, sweet juice.

(2) This time the mayonnaise is mixed with the roe (the orange and only edible part) of two sea-urchins, which will give a very distinctive flavour to the sauce. Since many of you reading this book live miles away from the sea, you may never have the opportunity of trying this version of Maltese sauce; however, it is prudent to point out that it is only the female sea-urchin that is edible, and on no account should sea-urchins be taken from polluted or semi polluted waters.

the female sea-urchin

Maltese sauce also goes very well with fine boiled vegetables, such as asparagus and artichokes.

Fritturi tal-Artikli
Sea-anemone Fritters

Artikli are the little brown and purple anemones which abound in pools of seawater just off the shore. They are prised out of their holes with a sharp pen-knife, usually by young children who take them home for their mothers to make these tiny appetizing fritters. The anemones are first rinsed, and then thrown into boiling water for about 1 minute, whereby they shrink somewhat in size. After draining, the anemones are dusted with flour and dipped into beaten egg which has been flavoured with some crushed garlic and chopped parsley, and then they are fried in hot oil and served with lemon wedges.

Pulpetti tal-Makku
Fish Fritters

These fritters are made with very small fish, commonly known as *makku*. These are not more than an inch long, almost transparent, and are eaten whole, without being gutted. The *makku* are first rinsed under some running water, sprinkled with coarse salt and allowed to drain in a colander. They are then tossed in flour and dipped in beaten egg flavoured with parsley and garlic, then taken out of this mixture, by the spoonful, and fried in oil till brown and crisp. They are served with lemon wedges and a crisp salad.

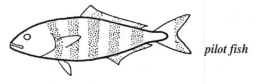

pilot fish

Stuffat tal-Fekruna
Turtle Stew/Soup

A Gozitan (Gozo is Malta's sister island) friend of mine, whose father was a fisherman, recalls how his mother used to make a stew with turtle meat and all sorts of delicious things like currants, peanuts, sultanas and even pieces of dark chocolate. This was then cooked on a *kenur* (see sketch on page 65), a primitive limestone stove, for a whole day! The turtle is now a protected species, and local fishermen return the turtles which accidentally get entangled in their nets to the sea. Up to the 1940's turtles used to come to shore to lay their eggs on certain sandy beaches such as Golden Bay in Malta and Ramla Bay in Gozo.

75

PULPETTI TAT-TONN TAZ-ZEJT
TUNNY FISH CROQUETTES

Pulpetti are usually made with beef (recipe page 56). Delicious *pulpetti* can be made however with tinned tuna fish instead of meat.

1 200g tin of tuna fish, 8 medium sized potatoes, 1 beaten egg, 1 grated onion, lots of chopped parsley, a few chopped capers, 2 crushed cloves of garlic, seasoning.

Boil and mash the potatoes. Drain the oil from the tuna, mix well with the mashed potatoes, and bind with the beaten egg. Add the parsley, the grated onion and the garlic, and season well with freshly ground black pepper and salt. With floured hands form ping-pong ball sized shapes, or slightly larger and flatter hamburger shapes from the mixture. Roll in flour and fry till golden in hot oil. Serve warm or cold with a fresh salad. This is a cheap and nourishing dish, ideal for children and toothless adults, or to take on picnics.

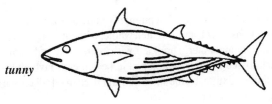

tunny

A short note on inkfish:-
Three members of the inkfish family are found in Maltese waters. Their name derives from the ink sac which they all possess, and from which ink is squirted to ward off enemies. The three differ slightly from one another, both in looks and in taste.

Cuttlefish *(sicca)*, is known mostly because of its back bone, which is often to be found washed up on the sea-shore, especially after storms. Cuttlefish bone is given to cage-birds to use as a sharpener for their beaks.

Squid *(klamari)* is probably best known to Northern Europeans who have visited the Mediterranean resorts in Spain and Greece, where it is cut into rings, deep fried and eaten with lemon or tartar sauce. In Malta we do not usually cook squid this way; instead, we stuff them with rice and herbs, and then stew them in wine. The body of the squid is elongated, the head proportionally much smaller, and the ten long tentacles very slim. The Maltese word for squid *(klamar)*, also means inkpot or inkstand!

Octopus *(qarnit)*, is the most popular with the Maltese. It is caught in abundance, just off our rocky shores. Octopus cannot be stuffed or deep fried as squid; its characteristics are the eight,

76

long, rather thick tentacles, lined with two rows of suckers each, which radiate from the large, round, central head. Beneath this head is a beak, similar to that of a budgerigar; its bite can be quite painful, to which I can testify, having been bitten by rather a large octopus some summers ago. The tentacles and most parts of the head are cut up and made into stews and sauces. Fresh squid and octopus are nowadays obtainable in most European cities.

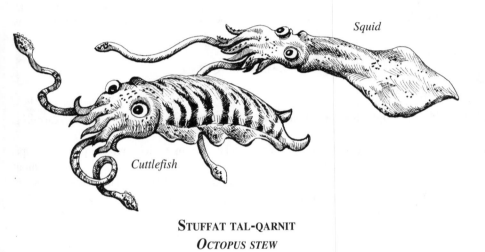

Squid

Cuttlefish

Stuffat tal-Qarnit
Octopus stew

1 kilo octopus (to serve five), 6 medium sized onions, 6 tomatoes, 12 small or 6 large potatoes, 8 cloves of garlic, 8 olives, a tablespoon of capers, a few leaves of marjoram and mint, a pinch of thyme, olive oil, red wine. Optional: sultanas, curry powder.

Clean the octopus by turning the head inside out and removing the insides. Cut away and discard the beak and the two eyes. The rest of the flesh is all edible. Place the octopus in a plastic bag and beat it with a meat hammer against the kitchen table. The real thing to do of course is to beat the octopus against the rocks when it has just been caught. This action tenderizes the flesh. Cut the octopus with a sharp knife into pieces about 5cm in length. Rinse them in salted water, and allow them to drain.

Place the pieces of octopus in a pot over a very low fire, and allow to stew for about an hour. The octopus will emit quite a lot of liquid, but if you think it's getting too dry, add a little hot water or white wine. In the meantime select the onions and tomatoes. Peel and chop the onions and fry

77

them in olive oil; as soon as they soften, add the peeled and chopped tomatoes. Crush the garlic, and add this too. When the tomatoes are softening, mix in all the herbs, the stoned and chopped olives, and the capers.

By this time, the octopus pieces are ready to join in. Increase the temperature to boiling, pour in 1/4 bottle of red wine, lower the heat and stew slowly till the liquid reduces considerably. Some cooks like to add a few sultanas and even curry powder, however, I find that this camouflages the real taste of the octopus. Serve octopus stew with lightly boiled small potatoes or else, go one better, by adding thick slices of raw potato and stewing them with the octopus.

Zalza tal-Qarnit
Octopus sauce for pasta

1/2 kilo of octopus, 3 onions, 3 tomatoes, a handful of peas, thyme or oregano, seasoning.

Clean, cut up (maximum 3cm) and stew the octopus in its own juices, as in the previous recipe. Fry the sliced onions in olive oil, adding the peeled and chopped tomatoes as soon as the onions begin to soften. Season with black pepper, freshly ground, and a pinch of the herbs. Simmer for a few minutes, then add the peas and the octopus pieces. Cook on a very low flame for a further 10 minutes.

Qarnit bl-Aljoli
Octopus with garlic

Octopus cooked in this way is usually eaten as an appetizer with drinks.

250g octopus, 4-6 cloves of crushed and chopped garlic, 1 bunch of finely cut parsley, 1 tablespoon olive oil, the juice of half a lemon, black pepper from the mill.

Clean and cut the octopus up into 2cm bits. Stew on its own or with a little white wine, as in the 2 preceding recipes. Drain the cooked octopus pieces, and mix well in a bowl with the rest of the ingredients. Keeps well in the fridge.

The octopus that did not want to get cooked

KLAMARI MIMLI FL-INBID
STUFFED SQUID STEWED IN WINE

12 small or 2 rather large squid (about 800g in all), the crumbs from 4 thick slices of white bread, 1 tablespoon capers, 4 stoned and chopped olives, 2 crushed cloves of garlic, a hint of grated lemon rind, a pinch of grated mace, 1 tablespoon of finely chopped parsley, 3 hard-boiled eggs, a bayleaf, a small handful of sultanas, a tumbler or two of good red wine, olive oil, seasoning.

Remove the insides, and long thin backbones; chop off, and having retained any tentacles which are to be used in the stuffing, discard the heads.

Rinse out the sacs with salted water. Make a stuffing with the breadcrumbs, the capers, the olives, the garlic, the parsley, the mace and the lemon rind. Season, bind with a few drops of olive oil, and mix in the chopped up tentacles.

Now fill the sacs up to 1/3 with stuffing, then with quarters of hard-boiled egg and more stuffing. The squid must not be filled to capacity, since they will contract somewhat during cooking. Sew up the openings with thread. Heat some oil in a large pan and give the squid a quick fry all over, together with the bayleaf. Pour the red wine over these, add the sultanas, cover properly, and stew slowly. Serve the stewed squid on beds of saffron rice, and pour the wine sauce from the pan over the rice.

KLAMARI MIMLI FIZ-ZALZA TAT-TADAM
STUFFED SQUID IN TOMATO SAUCE

12 small or 2 large squid (800g in all), 2 onions, 4 large peeled tomatoes, 1 handful of peas, 3 hard-boiled eggs, the crumbs from 4 slices of white bread without crusts, 6 stoned and finely chopped olives, 2 finely cut salted-anchovy fillets, 1 tablespoon of capers, fresh herbs, such as basil, mint and marjoram, salt, ground black pepper.

Prepare the squid as in the preceding recipe, retaining the tentacles for the sauce. Make the stuffing using the breadcrumbs, the olives, the anchovies, the capers, and any of the herbs you prefer. Season and bind with a few drops of olive oil. First brown the squid in a pan of hot olive oil, then put them aside and fry the diced onions in the same pan, eventually adding the chopped tomatoes and tentacles. Stir-fry for a few minutes and now return the whole squid to the pan, together with the peas. Pour in a glass of water, cover and stew slowly. The delicious sauce is eaten with spaghetti. The squid, after having slightly cooled down, are sliced into thickish rings and sprinkled with some olive oil. They can also be eaten with the spaghetti, as a side dish, or later, cold. *They taste exquisite.*

STUFFAT TAL-BAKKALJAW 1
SALT-COD STEW 1

Salt-cod used to, and still is, looked down upon by some people - it's considered poor man's fare. For those who really appreciate good food however, this is an ingenious way of preserving and cooking fish.

Imported salt-cod can be purchased from most supermarkets, and the delicatessen stalls at the Valletta market.

500g salt-cod, 2 onions, 1 small cauliflower, 1 large slice (200g) of pumpkin, 1/2 kilo potatoes, 6 peeled tomatoes, 8 stoned black olives, some mint leaves, 1 tiny hot red-pepper.

First soak the salt-cod overnight in plenty of water, then drain it and cut it into portion-sized pieces. Sweat the thinly sliced onions in olive oil and add the chopped tomatoes and the fish. After a few minutes of stir-frying, insert the olives, the pumpkin cut into largish cubes, the cauliflower florets, and the quartered potatoes. Top up with water, bring to the boil, and then simmer till the fish is cooked - the flesh will easily flake off the bones. At the very end mix in the finely chopped pepper. Watch out for bones!

STUFFAT TAL-BAKKALJAW 2
SALT- COD STEW 2

1/2 kilo salt-cod, 1 small onion, 1 carrot, 250g potatoes, 2 peeled tomatoes, 1 crushed clove of garlic, 1 tablespoon raisins, 2 finely chopped anchovy fillets, a few sprigs of parsley, black pepper - freshly ground, a pinch of nutmeg, olive oil.

After having soaked(overnight) and drained the fish, try and remove as many bones as possible, and then cut it up into smaller pieces. Heat some olive oil in a large pan and brown the sliced potatoes and carrot. Add the chopped tomatoes, the grated onion, the anchovy fillets and the garlic, and cook for 5 minutes. Now insert the fish and the raisins, pour in 1/4 litre water, stir, and spice up with the pepper and nutmeg. Cover the pan, and stew gently for about half an hour. Strew with chopped parsley, and bring to the table.

Maltese saying: donnu bakkaljawa.
Translation: he looks like a salt-cod; meaning, he is all skin and bones.

SFINEC TAL-INCOVA
ANCHOVY PUFFS

About 4 salted-anchovy fillets per person, 100g flour, 2 teaspoons baking powder, lemon wedges, sprigs of parsley, oil for frying, water.

Mix the flour with the baking powder and add enough water to make a smooth, runny batter. Dip the anchovy fillets into this batter and fry them immediately in plenty of very hot oil. Serve piping hot, sprinkled with lemon juice, and decorated with parsley. Also taste good dipped into mayonnaise or tartar sauce. *Sfinec* are usually served as a snack or with drinks.

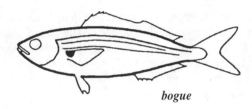

bogue

From a Maltese folk song:

Katarin gibtlek lampuka
Katarin kebbes in-nar
Katarin iftah it-tieqa
Halli johrog id-duhhan.

Translation:

Katarin I brought you a lampuka
Katarin kindle the fire
Katarin open the window
To let out the smoke.

SWEET THINGS

Maltese idiom: biskuttini f'halq il-hmir.
Translation: Sweetmeats in the mouth of a donkey; meaning, a good thing in the hands of a fool.

The vast number of religious feasts that occur in Malta coupled with the locals' love of any type of celebration, have seen to it that sweets are not lacking on the national menu. Visit any village on the day of the feast of its patron saint, and you will find the streets lined with colourful stalls offering sweets, purposely made for the occasion. There are special sweets for baptisms, and others for weddings; sweets not only for Christmas time and Easter, but even for Carnival and Lent.

Imbuljata
Chestnut Soup

Unusual to find a recipe for a soup in the chapter on sweets! Hot chestnut soup is traditionally eaten on Good Friday, when the processions, which take place in many towns and villages, have come to an end.

400g dried and peeled chestnuts, rind of 1 tangerine (or orange) and of 1 lemon, a 2cm stick of cinnamon, 4 cloves, 100g cocoa powder, 200g brown sugar.

Soak the peeled chestnuts overnight. Drain, change the water, bring to the boil and add all the remaining ingredients. Lower the flame, and simmer slowly till the chestnuts are tender to the bite. Remove the tangerine and lemon rinds, the cloves and the cinnamon, and serve the soup in individual cups or bowls. For a stronger version, lace with dark rum or aniseed liqueur.

Biskuttini tal-Maghmudija
Biscuits for a Christening

8 eggs, 800g flour, 800g sugar, 60g candied peel, 1/2 a teaspoon each of ground cloves and cinnamon, 1 teaspoon bicarbonate of soda, icing sugar, food colouring - sky blue, pink, pale yellow and green.

Separate the egg whites from the yolks. First beat the whites quite stiff, then mix in the yolks. Add the very finely chopped candied peel, the sugar, the bicarbonate, the spices and finally the flour which should be folded in gradually. Butter a sheet of grease-proof paper, and sprinkle with a little flour and caster sugar. Spread this out on your baking tray. Now flour the palms of your hands, and taking a dessert-spoon of mixture at a time, form small round, flattish biscuits, laying them out in well spaced rows on the baking sheet. Bake in a hot oven for around 10 minutes, by which time they should be done, but not burnt. Coat the biscuits with an extremely thin layer of white icing, and decorate with icing curls and spirals of various colours - traditionally blue for boys, and pink for girls.

MQARET
DATE-FILLED PIES

These are very popular sweet snacks which are sold from street stalls in certain towns - City Gate at Valletta, for example, where you can actually observe the vendor at his stall, frying the *mqaret* in huge cauldrons of boiling oil.

For the pastry: 450g flour, 110g margarine, 1 tablespoon sugar, a few drops of aniseed liqueur, a few drops of orange-blossom water.
For the filling: 360g stoned dates, a pinch of ground cloves, shredded tangerine and lemon or orange peel, 1 tablespoon aniseed liqueur, 1 tablespoon orange-blossom water.

Cut up the margarine into small pieces and rub these into the flour which you have sieved into a large bowl. Add the sugar and blend well, moistening with the liqueur and orange-blossom water. Chop the dates and soak in very little water for half an hour, then cook them in a saucepan for just 5 minutes. Pour off any excess liquid, and add the remaining ingredients for the filling; mix these well together. Roll the pastry out into a strip 10cm in width. Moisten the edges of the pastry strip, and spoon the date mixture down its middle; fold over, enclosing the date filling, and pressing the edges tightly together. Using a sharp knife, cut diagonally across the pastry into 5cm long diamond-shaped *mqaret*. Deep fry the *mqaret* in boiling oil till golden brown, drain, and serve piping hot.

Figolli
Easter figures

At Easter time all the shops are selling *figolli*. In recent years *figolli* sales have toppled those for Easter eggs, so despite outside influence, this tradition lives on. The children expect to get a *figolla* or two not only from their parents but also grandparents and aunts.

The *figolla* is a decorative sweet pastry filled with marzipan, and shaped prettily as teddy bears, swans, lambs, bunnies, fish, mermaids and hearts amongst others.

The metal forms or shapes (about 18cm long), with which the pastry is cut, can be purchased from most confectioneries and household shops.

For the pastry: 400g margarine, 800g flour, 200g sugar, 3 egg yolks, 1/2 a teaspoon grated lemon rind, water.
For the filling: 400g each of sugar and almonds, a dessertspoon of orange-blossom water, the 3 egg whites.

Sieve the flour into a large bowl and using the tips of your fingers rub the margarine into the flour till it resembles fine breadcrumbs. Sweeten this with the sugar, and spice up with the lemon rind. Mix in the egg yolks and enough water required to make a stiffish dough. In the meantime prepare the filling, by grinding the sugar together with the almonds, adding the orange-blossom water, and folding the beaten egg-whites into this mixture. Dust your table-top with flour and roll out the pastry. Using the metal shapes, cut out 2 similar shapes for each single *figolla*. If you do not happen to have any of these metal shapes, use your immagination and artistic skill! Now spread a thick (1cm) layer of the almond filling onto half of the pastry shapes lying on your table, leaving a bit of space (1cm) around the edges, and cover each one with its corresponding half; push the edges slightly together and bake for half an hour in a moderate oven. Allow to cool, and decorate with colourful icing or molten chocolate.

Maltese schoolchildrens' rhyme:
I am
thou art - figolla
he is - kielili kolla.

Translation:
I am
thou art - figolla
he is - he ate it all up.

Kannoli
Ricotta filled pastries

These can best be described as deep fried pastry tubes which are filled with sweetened ricotta.

For the pastry: 3 tablespoons of lard, 400g flour, 3 tablespoons caster sugar, 2 beaten egg yolks, a little white wine.
For the filling: 400g ricotta, 4 tablespoons sugar, 2 tablespoons honey, 75g each of chopped chocolate and candied fruit, 50g chopped roasted nuts (pistachios, walnuts or hazelnuts), a pinch of cinnamon and a few drops of vanilla essence.

Sieve the flour into a large bowl and rub the lard into it as described in the previous recipe. Sweeten this mixture with the caster sugar. Add the egg yolks, and enough of the wine to make a dough. Knead and allow to rest for 1 hour. Now roll out the pastry as thinly as possible. To shape the *kanolli* we use special metal tubes of about 9cm in length and 2cm in diameter, which can be purchased from some household shops; the outer surface of these tubes is greased with oil, and the pastry cut out and rolled around each one of them. They are then fried in oil until the pastry gets nice and golden. If you are skilful enough, you can shape the *kannoli* using your hands, without using the metal tubes. The pastry tubes are now allowed to drip and cool, and then gently removed from their tin shapes. Now, blend the ricotta with the rest of the ingredients to make a sweet filling, and stuff the *kannoli* with this. Roll in icing sugar, and keep in the fridge till eating time!

Qaghaq tal-Gunglien
Sesame Rings

460g self-raising flour, 230g margarine, 200g white sugar, 1 egg, juice and grated rind of 1 lemon, 3 tablespoons of whole sesame seeds.

Using your finger-tips rub the margarine into the flour till it is fully absorbed. Mix in the sugar, the beaten egg, and eventually the lemon juice. Knead into a compact dough. Flour the palms of your hands, and break off small pieces from the dough, about the size of a golf ball. Form these, by rubbing up and down between the palms of both hands, into elongated 1.5cm thick shapes; now curl these into rings, spirals and figures of eight. Place on a floured baking tray, strew with the sesame seeds, and bake in a hot oven for 25 minutes.

KWAREZIMAL
LENTEN SWEETMEAT

This sweetmeat contains neither fat nor eggs, and was traditionally eaten during Lent, when rather strict fasting regulations existed upto about three decades ago. Even nowadays *kwarezimal* is still made at Lent, but most of all because it is so delicious.

400g flour, 400g brown sugar, 400g roasted and ground almonds, 1/2 a teaspoon each of ground cinnamon and ground cloves, the grated rind of 1 lemon and of 1 orange or tangerine, 1 tablespoon cocoa powder, 1 tablespoon orange-blossom water.
To decorate with: honey, chopped almonds or pistachios.

Sift the flour into a large bowl, and combine well with all the other ingredients. Add just a very little water to form a stiff dough. Take pieces from the dough and form into shapes about 15cm in length, 5cm in width and 1.5cm thick. Space the pieces out onto a floured baking tray, and bake in a moderate oven for about 20 minutes, or till the dough is no longer soft. Allow to cool somewhat, smear with good honey, and sprinkle with chopped almonds or pistachios. Some of the commercial varieties I have tried do not taste at all like the genuine thing.

TORTA TAL-MARMURATA
RICH ALMOND TART

For the pastry: 200g flour, 100g margarine, 2 dessertspoons sugar, 1 egg yolk.
For the filling: 200g minced almonds, 200g chopped candied peel, 100g sugar, 3 eggs, 1/2 a teaspoon of cinnamon, 50g grated dark chocolate.

Sift the flour into a large bowl. With the tips of your fingers rub the fat in to the flour till it is completely absorbed. Combine with the sugar, the egg yolk, and enough water required to make a dough. Let it rest, and in the meantime prepare the filling. Beat the eggs, add the sugar and continue beating. Fold in the almonds, the candied peel, the cinnamon and the chocolate. Line a greased baking tin with the pastry, ladle the filling evenly on to the pastry, and bake in a moderate oven for about 40 minutes. Bring out the *torta*, allow it to cool and finally coat it with a thin layer of molten dark chocolate. This is an absolutely delicious and very presentable sweet, ideal for bridge parties and high teas.

Qubbajt
Maltese nougat

I do not know of anyone who actually makes this sweet at home; it is usually manufactured by certain confectioners on a commercial basis, and sold from the attractive sweet stalls at the village festas. *Qubbajt* is the feast day sweetmeat.

It is made of sugar, glucose, honey and egg white, all of which are heated to a certain temperature and then mixed with almonds and candied fruit, and allowed to cool. The secret lies not only in the taste, but also in the consistency. *Qubbajt* must never be too hard that it cannot be bitten into, but yet it must be firm and not too soft. *Qubbajt* is sold in rectangular blocks of various size, sometimes even rolled into cigar-shaped cylinders, wrapped first in rice paper and then in colourful foil.

Gulepp tal-Harrub
Carob syrup

The carob is a hardy tree which grows all over the islands of Malta and Gozo. Nature has perfectly adapted these trees to life on a windy island. The carob never grows to great heights; instead it branches outwards and downwards, its branches and twigs thus forming an umbrella-shaped protection to the main trunk. Carob trees have a long life, and there are some beautiful specimens around which surely remember the times of the Knights of Malta!

1 kilo dried carob pods, 1 kilo sugar, water.

The carob pods must be picked at the end of the season, when they are quite dry and black. First roast the carob pods in a hot oven, then cut them up into pieces, and soak in plenty of water for 24 hours. Now boil them slowly for about 1 hour, by which time the juices from the pods would have been drawn out, and the water become dark. Pass the contents of the pot through a sieve and return to the fire with the addition of the sugar. Stir well to dissolve the sugar, bring to the boil and simmer for 1 1/2 hours. The result is a thick dark syrup which can be stored in sterilized jars or bottles. A spoonful of carob extract diluted with hot water is recommended as a natural cough syrup.

BAJTAR TAX-XEWK
PRICKLY PEARS

The *opuntia ficus indica* (prickly pear) is the commonest true cactus of the Mediterranean region. It is originally a tropical plant and is believed to have been imported to Europe by Christopher Columbus. I have decided to include a short note on this fruit in the sweets chapter, because it is such a typical feature of the Maltese countryside. Flowering early in summer in brilliant yellow and orange its brick-red and purple fruits are available up to November. Sometimes foreigners ask me if marmalade is ever made from the prickly pear, apparently this being done in Spain. I've never heard of this in Malta.

Recently I watched a Californian chef on television preparing a meal from the large thick leaves of the prickly pear cactus! This should be something for some adventurous Maltese cook to experiment with, but till then I'm afraid no local version is available.

The oval almost egg-shaped prickly pears are so popular in Malta because they are cheap and refreshing, especially after having lain in the fridge for some hours. To be quite honest, I find the taste rather bland and only slightly sweet. The fruits are usually placed in a bucket of water so that the tiny fine thorns which cover them become soft and easier to handle. Usually the vendor himself peels the prickly pears for his customers; these then take the fruits home in their own dish or bowl.

PUDINA TAL-HOBZ
BREADPUDDING

This is a simple, cheap but delicious dessert.

500g of 2 days old white bread, 1/4 litre milk, 1 glass dark rum, 3 beaten eggs, 100g sultanas, 50g candied orange peel, grated rind of 1 lemon, 3 tablespoons cocoa powder, 3 tablespoons sugar, 1/2 teaspoon cinnamon, 50g butter.

Soak the bread slices overnight in the milk and rum, squeeze out, and retain the liquid. Cut the bread up roughly, and mix well in a bowl with the rest of the ingredients excepting the butter. Grease an oven-proof ceramic or pyrex dish with butter, transfer the bread mixture into this, pour the liquid (milk and rum) over it, and finally top up with little knobs of butter. Bake in a moderate to low oven. The bread pudding will be ready when a sharp knife passes clean through it. Serve warm or cold.

PRINJOLATA
PINE-NUT SWEETMEAT

This is the traditional carnival-time sweet. During carnival week (usually in February), pretty *prinjolata* "mountains" decorate every cafe and confectionery window.

150g butter, 320g caster sugar, 12 slices, about 3cm thick, of plain Madeira cake, 1 egg white, a couple of drops of vanilla essence, 50g each of: roasted and ground pine-nuts, whole pine-nuts, halved candied cherries, grated dark chocolate.

With your electric mixer, blend the butter and 200g of the sugar to a smooth cream. Beat the egg-white in a bowl which you have placed in a hotwater bath. Keep beating, and at the same time add the rest of the sugar(120g), 1/2 a tumbler of water, and the drops of vanilla. Remove from the fire, allow to cool, and carefully fold into the creamed butter together with the crushed pine-nuts.

Grease a pudding basin, and layer alternately to the top with the cake slices which you have halved horizontally, and the sweetened creamed butter mixture. Let this stay overnight in the fridge. Now turn the *prinjolata* carefully out of its container and decorate with the whole pine-nuts, the chocolate flakes and the cherries. The *prinjolata* will resemble a little snow-capped mountain.

BISKUTTINI TAL-QASTAN
CHESTNUT BISCUITS

400g whole chestnuts, 200g each of sugar, flour, and unsalted butter, 3 eggs, zest of 1 lemon.

Peel the chestnuts from both their skins, and boil them till they are soft. Having drained them, mash them with a potato masher, and then pass them through a sieve (or puree them in a food processor). Add the butter, the sugar, the sifted flour and the lemon zest. Mix these ingredients together and then add the egg yolks. Knead to a dough, and then take pieces not bigger than a ping-pong ball and roll between the palms of your hands to form the cigar-shaped biscuits. Brush these over with the beaten egg-whites, and bake for about 25 minutes in a moderate oven.

BISKUTTINI TAL-LEWZ
ALMOND MACAROONS

300g ground almonds, 100g caster sugar, 2 egg-whites, a few blanched whole almonds, a sheet of rice paper.

Beat the egg-whites stiff, then add the sugar and beat again. Fold in the ground almonds. Take teaspoons of the mixture and arrange in rows on the rice paper which you have placed on a greased baking tray. Decorate each macaroon with a whole almond. Bake for about 20 minutes in a moderate oven. The macaroons will almost double in size during baking, so they should be spaced well apart.

PUDINA TAT-TAMAL
FIG PUDDING

Around Christmas time, there are lots of dried figs in the shops. We like to eat them with nuts after a heavy lunch. This is a nice recipe for turning these simple fruits into a splendid dessert.

200g dried figs, 200g breadcrumbs, 100g caster sugar, 100g candied orange peel, 4 eggs, 2 tablespoons of aniseed liqueur.

Chop the dried figs rather finely, and mix them in a bowl with the breadcrumbs, the sugar, and the candied orange cut small. Beat the eggs, and bind with the other ingredients in the bowl.

Butter a pudding basin, and fill it with this mixture up to 2cm from the upper rim. Cover the top with a buttered round of grease-proof paper, wrap up the basin tightly in a white tea-towel, and secure with a piece of string. Now place the pudding-basin in a cold water-bath up to 3/4 of the way up, bring to the boil, lower the flame and allow to simmer gently for 2 hours. Test the pudding with a knitting needle, which should come out clean. Turn out the pudding onto a large dish and douse it with the liqueur. Serve hot or cold.

Qaghaq tal-Ghasel
Honey or treacle rings

For the pastry: 400g flour, 75g semolina, 100g unsalted butter, 1 egg yolk, a tablespoon of sugar, some water.
For the filling: 400g treacle, 150g sugar, grated rind of an orange or tangerine, and a lemon, a tablespoon of chopped candied fruit, a pinch of cloves, a tablespoon of cocoa and one of aniseed liqueur, a little semolina, 2 cups of water.

The pastry can be made beforehand and kept in the fridge. Sieve the flour into a bowl with the semolina, rub in the butter, mix in the egg-yolk and sugar and knead well to form a smooth dough. Add water if necessary.

Mix together all the ingredients for the filling (except the semolina); bring slowly to the boil in a saucepan, simmer gently, and start adding the semolina till you get a thickish consistency, taking care to stir the mixture constantly.

Roll the pastry out thinly and cut out several 20cm x 6cm rectangles. Take spoonfuls of the filling, form into cigar-shaped strips and place down the middle of your pastry rectangles. First roll the pastry over the filling Swiss-roll fashion, then bring the two ends together to form a circle or ring. At intervals of a few centimetres cut little slits into the pastry.

Place the rings on a floured baking tray and bake in a moderate oven till the pastry starts to get some colour. You will find that some of the treacle filling will have come out through the slits in the pastry making attractive black and white rings

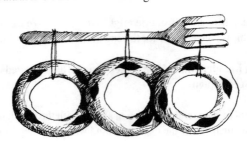

Laring tal-bakkaljaw
Orange marmalade

750g Seville oranges, 1.5 kilos sugar, 1 lemon, 3 litres of water.

Peel the oranges and the lemon, and cut up the peel into thin strips. Remove the pips from the fruit and place them in a small piece of muslin cloth. Chop up the flesh of the fruit, and place in a pan with the water together with the strips of rind. Tie up the muslin cloth to form a tiny bag, and insert into the pan. Boil till the peel is tender, and the liquid reduced to about half (approximately 2 hours). Remove the muslin bag, squeezing out any liquid back into the pan. Add the sugar, and bring gently to the boil. Increase the heat, and whilst stirring occasionally allow to bubble for half an hour. Test with a teaspoon; it should have the consistency of very thick honey. Allow to cool slightly and pour into sterilized jars. Exquisite breakfast fare.

Hawh
Peach jam

1 kilo of stoned peaches, 1 kilo of sugar.

Wash the peaches very well, and remove the stones. Do not peel. Weigh the stoned peaches, and take the same amount in weight of sugar. Cut up the peaches and place them in a pan together with the sugar. Cook slowly until the sugar melts and then increase the heat. Allow to bubble for about 30 minutes. Pour into sterilized jars.

Sweet rice a la Malta

Despite the name, this is not a Maltese dish. I came across it in Sweden where it occurs quite regularly on restaurant menus. In 1980 I was working at a resort in Halmstad on the south coast of Sweden. It was Christmas Eve, and we were preparing a luncheon for three hundred guests. This was to be in the typically Swedish *smorgasbord* fashion. All the cooks were given a particular dish to prepare. Since I was Maltese, it was decided that I should be the one to make the dessert, *Ris a la Malta,* as they call it. When the hectic work in the kitchen was over, we cooks gathered in our corner, savouring some of the delicacies we had prepared that morning: pickled herrings, exquisite salmon, meatballs, spare ribs, succulent hams and savoury cheeses - everything that has made the Swedish *smorgasbord* famous worldwide. All of a sudden the

kitchen door burst open wide; the head chef charged in like a mad woman:
"Where's the boy from Malta? Where's the lad from Malta? You fool" she yelled, "you ruined the dessert, the guests are all complaining, you put salt with the rice instead of sugar!"
"Fool?" I retorted, stubborn as I was in those days, "whose the fool? we always put salt with the rice in Malta!"

I never kept the exact ingredients for *Ris a la Malta,* but it is done in the following way: Pudding rice is first cooked in milk together with a whole vanilla pod and caster sugar. When the mixture cools down, it is mixed with whipped cream, and orange or tangerine segments.

Maltese idiom: Jekk trid il-haga maghmula sewwa ghamilha int.
Translation: If you want a task done properly, best do it yourself.

A FINAL WORD

"Maltese cooking is on the whole undistinguished."

Malta: An Archaeological Guide, by D.H. Trump, Faber and Faber 1972.

Hopefully, those of you who have by now read my book and tried out some of the recipes, will have come to the conclusion that the good Doctor's assertion above, is quite incorrect.

List of Recipes

Soups

Pasta, Rice and Savoury Pies

Vegetables and Salads

CHICKEN, RABBIT, SNAILS AND GAME

FISH, OCTOPUS AND EVERYTHING THAT COMES FROM THE SEA

SWEET THINGS